From the
Global Kitchen

A Collection of
Vegetarian Recipes
by **Plenty International**

© Plenty International 1995

Cover by Page/Curtis
Interior design by Sheryl Karas

Printed in the United States by Book Publishing Company
PO Box 99
Summertown, TN 38483

From the global kitchen: a collection of vegetarian recipes / by Plenty International
  [Charles Thomas Haren, editor].
        p.   cm.
    Includes index
    ISBN   1-57067-006-4 (paperback)

  1. Vegetarian cookery.   2. Cookery, International.   I. Haren.
Charles Thomas, 1951-   . II. Plenty International (Organization)
  TX837.V4269   1995
641.5'636--dc20   95-14033
                                                        CIP

Calculations for the nutritional analyses in this book are based on the average number of servings listed with the recipes and the average amount of an ingredient if a range is called for. Calculations are rounded up to the nearest gram. If two options for an ingredient are listed, the first one is used. Not included are fat used for frying, unless the amount is specified in the recipe, optional ingredients, or servings suggestions.

Acknowledgments

A special thanks to all individuals, community groups, and organizations Plenty has worked with in adapting the use of soyfoods to traditional family diets, without whom we would not have such imaginative recipes, or rewarding experiences to share. To Chuck Haren, who collected and refined many of the recipes during his years of soy promotion work: to Lisa Wartinger and Peter Schweitzer for keeping the ball rolling: to Michael Cook, Barbara Bloomfield, and Jerry Hutchens from the Book Publishing Company, who put in many hours of work testing recipes, doing the nutritional analyses, editing, layout, and numerous other tasks preparing this book for print: and to the Plenty volunteers who had the presence of mind to take these beautiful photographs, we express our appreciation.

Thanks also to John Robbins, Louise Hagler, and Virginia and Mark Messina, for their encouragement, and to Plenty's Board of Directors for keeping the vision alive. Special thanks to Plenty's kind and faithful donors, without whom none of this would be possible. Thanks to the people of the Farm, past and present, for their courage and commitment, and to the noble soybean, long may it prosper.

Contents

Foreword by Virginia & Mark Messina

In China it is called *ta tou*, which means "greater bean," and throughout all of Asia, the soybean is viewed with a certain amount of reverence. It's small wonder. In a world with limited arable land and a growing population, soybeans, efficiently produced, packed with nutrition, and incredibly versatile, are of great importance to the human diet.

The versatility of the soybean is nothing short of amazing. In its mature state, it is eaten as a legume or dried bean. Immature green soybeans are a fantastic vegetable. And ancient soy foods like tofu, tempeh, and soymilk have given rise to an endless variety of products that easily and deliciously replace dairy and meat products in the diet. Whatever foods you like, from frosty, fruity milk shakes or chocolaty desserts, to savory, barbecued cutlets or cheesy, stuffed pasta dishes, there is a role for soy in your diet. Soy is at home in every kind of dish imaginable.

Our own interest has been in the nutritional properties of soybeans, which are nothing short of incredible. Soybeans are rich in high quality protein, calcium, iron, and vitamins, but that is just the beginning of the good news about soy. Today, scientists are investigating soybeans for promising roles in the prevention and/or treatment of heart disease, cancer, osteoporosis, and kidney disease.

An impressive number of studies conducted over the past 25 years show that soy protein directly lowers blood cholesterol levels when soy replaces animal protein in the diet. On average, blood cholesterol levels drop by 12 percent which can decrease heart disease risk by as much as 25 percent.

Soybeans also contain substances which posses anticancer activity. At least one of these, called *genistein*, is unique to soybeans. If you want to consume this cancer-fighting compound, you have to eat soy foods. Genistein stops the growth of cancer cells in the laboratory and also inhibits tumors in studies of experimental cancer. Not surprisingly, Japanese people who eat soy foods regularly have a lower rate of cancer than Japanese people who eat soy foods infrequently. As little as one serving of soy foods a day may be enough to decrease cancer risk.

Soybeans also promote bone health. In addition to being an excellent source of well-absorbed calcium, the protein in soy is easier on your bones than protein from milk and other animal foods. Animal protein increases the loss of calcium from bones. Soy protein is equal in nutritional quality to animal protein, but doesn't have this calcium-wasting effect. In addition, other substances in soy may directly inhibit bone loss. Finally, diets high in soy protein may help to prevent or treat kidney disease. Researchers have recommended that soy be included in the diets of kidney patients.

But of all the exciting news about soybeans, perhaps the most important is this: soybeans are among the best foods for feeding an overcrowded planet. As the world's population grows and agricultural land becomes more scarce, we need to turn to crops that fulfill three criteria. First, they must be easily grown, producing significant amounts of protein on small amounts of land. Second, they must be extremely nutritious. And third, they must be versatile and useful in the diets of many cultures. Soybeans fit these criteria more easily than any other crop.

But soyfoods aren't just for people who live where food is scarce. Eating lower on the food chain, that is, eating meals based on plant foods, is one important way we can all see to it that there is enough to go around. You don't have to include soy products in your menus to eat a plant-based diet, but they make it especially easy and fun to eat this way.

From the Global Kitchen offers some exciting cooking on two counts. First, it's a great introduction to soy foods if you aren't already familiar with these products. Second, it offers these foods packaged in a variety of wonderful, international cuisines, truly some of the world's best cooking. While people from Asia perfected soy foods, these foods are enjoying new lives in the cultures of other lands. Based on their nutritional and economic value, as well as their versatility, soy foods are appearing in the cuisines of countries throughout the world.

These recipes will undoubtedly improve your health. They go easy on the planet's resources. It's no small bonus that they are fun and delicious too!

Mark Messina, Ph.D.
Virginia Messina, MPH, RD
Authors, *The Simple Soybean and Your Health*

Introduction

The book you hold in your hands is part of a long, adventurous journey.

In the early 1970s, a group of committed, social and spiritual pioneers settled a 1,750 acre piece of land in rural Tennessee. Called simply The Farm, this territory became home to an extended family of friends whose intent and motivation was to make a positive impact on the world.

The challenge was this: to establish and promote a simple, but graceful life-style that was not overconsumptive, and that would conceivably be in reach of just about anyone, no matter where they were born. Meeting the challenge required developing a diet that was healthful and inexpensive to produce, and tasty enough that people would enjoy eating it. This led us to the wonders of the soybean—a protein "super source" with unique versatility.

Our early relationship with soyfoods involved cooking and eating the bean itself—in tortillas, over rice, or mashed, spiced, and fried as burgers. Over the years, more sophisticated uses of the bean were developed, and a soy "dairy" was built which produced enough soymilk, tofu, yogurt, "ice bean" (soy ice cream), and tempeh to help feed a community population that grew to more than 1,200 people.

Meanwhile, in another part of the world . . . The ancient and modern cultures of Guatemala were dealt a cataclysmic blow in 1976 when a devastating earthquake rocked that Central American country. In rural Mayan territory, houses constructed of heavy adobe brick and roofed with clay tiles proved deadly to many thousands who were sleeping when the *terremoto* struck in the middle of the night. Hearing of the disaster via firsthand reports broadcast by ham radio operators, our community held an emergency meeting to plan a response. In 1974, The Farm had conceived and incorporated a nonprofit organization called Plenty as the community's charitable arm. We began sending medical and construction crews to help those living in the hardest hit areas of Guatemala.

What started out as short term disaster relief soon became something much larger. As crews worked on the immediate crisis at hand, a less dramatic yet more insidious calamity became evident. The Mayan people, once masters of mathematics, astronomy, and architecture, suffer a depth of poverty which causes a cruel cycle of malnutrition, illness, and death. Mayan families, representing more than 60% of Guatemala's population, have been politically oppressed and economically marginalized since the time of the Spanish conquest. The average Guatemalan *campesinos* simply cannot produce enough to feed their families, on the limited amount of available land.

While rebuilding efforts continued and relationships with the local population grew, Mayan mothers began coming to Plenty's volunteer camp seeking help for their malnourished babies and young children. With an adequate diet which included soy milk, many of these babies began thriving. This led to a strong interest in this unusual, milk-giving bean. With Plenty's help, farmers experimented with growing soybeans, and hundreds of families learned to make soymilk and tofu in their homes. In 1980, Plenty and Mayan volunteers built a community owned soy dairy in the village of San Bartolo, near Solola. Local families, working at what is now called *Alimentos San Bartolo* (San Bartolo Foods), began producing soymilk, tofu, and soy ice cream and offering these nutritious and inexpensive foods to nearby communities.

Word of the success of the Guatemala soy program brought inquiries from people in many countries seeking information and technical assistance for similar projects. Since that first international effort, Plenty has been helping people around the world adapt soyfoods to their traditional diets.

Which brings us to this book. ***From the Global Kitchen*** is a collection of new and traditional recipes devised by some of the many people Plenty has worked with over the years. It is a sampling of how the incredible soybean has been incorporated into the tastes and cooking habits of a variety of cultures. We hope that you will enjoy the many original, healthful, and delicious recipes awaiting discovery in this cookbook and that you, too, will be inspired to join the adventure and create your own favorite vegetarian dishes.

Bon appetit, buen provecho, kishway, and good eating!

Lisa Wartinger - Plenty Chairwoman

Chuck Haren - Director of Plenty's Soy Utilization Program

Locating Ingredients

Cooking Tools

Many of the recipes included in this cookbook are commonly used by people living in the tropical and semitropical regions of the world. All of the original ingredients can be found at Asian, Caribbean, Latin American, or International food stores. Many of the ingredients are now also available at many large supermarkets. We suggest you try to locate the original ingredients, rather than using the suggested substitutes, in order to experience the full flavor of the original recipe.

baking pans - small - 4 x 8-inch and medium - 9 x 12-inch

blender - for mixing wet ingredients (32 ounce or larger)

coffee grinder - for grinding dry roasted soybeans for coffee and some spices

frying pans or skillets - small , medium, and large (diameter more than 12 inches)

hand mill - for grinding corn, wheat, or rice into grits or flour, some spices, and some cooked ingredients

meat grinder - to replace a murukku mold when making some Sri Lankan foods, and for grinding cooked soybeans

murukku mold - a mold used in Sri Lanka for making small round noodles; can be purchased where India and Sri Lankan foods are sold

pittu bamboo steamer - for steaming rice; can be purchased at Indian and Asian food specialty stores

sauce pans and pots - small (2-3 cups), medium (4-8 cups), and large (more than 8 cups)

steamer pot - one that has a perforated insert that allows you to steam what you are cooking without submerging it in water

Description of Uncommon Ingredients

Because many of these ingredients need a description or explanation and are listed in several recipes, we have included them here.

banana leaves: The green leaves from the banana tree are commonly rinsed and used for transporting food, cooking, and as plates for eating. They are also used for wrapping foods before steaming or baking.
substitute: canna leaves or corn husks

breadnut: The fruit from the breadnut tree, which grows in tropical regions. These soft edible nuts are normally roasted or boiled in water, and salted. When they are cooked and shelled, the nuts are soft and have a texture similar to small, slightly boiled white potatoes.
substitutes: chestnuts, new potatoes

breadfruit: A round tropical fruit from large trees, they are normally roasted or boiled.
substitute: potatoes

calalou: The young green leaf shoots from the dasheen plant grow in the Caribbean, Africa, and other tropical regions
substitutes: spinach or young collard greens

cassava (manioc or yucca): A root crop originating in South America that is now a staple in many parts of the world. Known as yucca in Central America, and manioc in parts of South America, cassava is starchy and low in protein. It must be boiled before being eaten.
substitute: white yams or large white potatoes

cassava flour: Flour made from the cassava plant.

chayote: Called christofeen in the Caribbean, the chayote has a unique starchy texture, and a pleasant taste. It is a green, pear-shaped squash that is popular in Central America and the Caribbean. Remove the large seed from the center, and use as you would any squash.
substitutes: young cucumber in salads and zucchini in cooked foods

coconut meal: The grated meat of the coconut that remains after the milk is squeezed out.

coconut milk: The liquid from blended, pressed, and strained coconut meat. Coconut milk can be purchased in small cans. It is similar in thickness to evaporated milk.

corn masa: A dough made from ground corn, lime, and water. Masa can be used for tortillas, tamales, and other Central American foods.

custard apple: Also called cherimoya, custard apples are a member of the Anona family. They are a very sweet, fleshy fruit grown in tropical regions. Custard apples are ripe when soft to the touch. Remove the seeds.
substitute: ripe peaches or plums

curry leaves: These leaves have the flavor of a curry mix and are commonly used in Sri Lanka and India.
substitute: curry powder

dasheen: A large tuber grown in tropical regions and used extensively in the Caribbean. The roots become grayish or violet when cooked.
substitute: white potatoes or white yams

dry corn: Also called field corn, these dry kernels are grown for meal, flour, and cereals. They are not the same varieties as sweet corn.

field corn (green): Field corn that is picked fresh after the kernels are fully developed, but before they dry out.

full fat soy flour: Fresh soy flour without the oil being extracted. Because of the oil content, it must be refrigerated to preserve its freshness.

green bananas: Fully developed but unripe bananas.

green chilies: These can be any variety of small fresh hot peppers.

groundnuts: This is the Caribbean name for peanuts.

guava: A unique tropical fruit commonly used in drinks and baked sweets. Guava has a tart taste and can be pink, white, or yellow.
substitutes: apricots or peaches.

harina: The Spanish word for flour.

jaggery (kitul): An unrefined, hardened molasses and sugar substance.
substitute: brown sugar

mace: A tropical spice made from the husk of nutmeg.

mango: A delicious, sweet, fleshy tropical fruit.

manioc (see cassava): The South American name for the cassava or yucca plant.

masa harina: A type of corn flour used in Latin American cooking. Best when it is freshly ground, masa harina can also be purchased as a packaged flour mix of the same name. Mixed with water, masa harina makes corn masa dough.

mirin: A sweet rice wine, mirin is frequently used in cooking. The alcohol evaporates during cooking but the sweet taste remains. It can be found in Asian grocery stores and some supermarkets.

murukku: A mixture of flours and spices that are made into a dough, pressed into round noodle shapes, and fried crisp for snack food.

nutritional yeast: A delicious food flavoring and seasoning, grown on molasses. It is high in B vitamins, protein, and essential amino acids. Nutritional yeast is not the same as brewer's yeast. It has a golden color, a mild, cheesy flavor, and comes in both flake and powder form. We recommended the flakes for the recipes in this cookbook. It can be purchased at health food stores.

oil: We recommend using a monounsaturated, non-hydrogenated vegetable oil such as olive or canola oil.

okara: The pulp that is left over after making soymilk or tofu. It is a white, fluffy meal that is high in fiber and has some protein. Okara has almost no flavor of its own, so it is adaptable to many types of dishes.
substitute: grated tofu

pigeon peas: A small green or red pea grown on a small treelike bush, common to tropical regions.
substitute: dry green peas or red cow peas

pinole: A type of flour that is made from roasted, dry corn.
substitute: toasted corn meal or flour

powdered soymilk: Dried soymilk can be used like dried cow's milk. It is available in health food stores in regular and low-fat varieties.

ranchero cheese: Also called queso fresco, it is a firm, white cow's milk cheese used in Mexico and Central America. It can be purchased in many supermarkets in the Latin American fresh food section, or in any Latin American food store.
substitute: any mild flavored, lightly salted cheese

ricado: A spicy, red poultry seasoning made from paprika, chili powder, and corn masa.

sapodilla: A very sweet, rich, strong-flavored fruit grown in Central America. They are a little grainy but very delicious. The seeds should always be removed.
substitute: large, ripe, sweet plums

sea moss (carrageenan or Irish moss): It is used as a thickening and solidifying agent and must be heated to 140°F to dissolve.

soursop: A tropical fruit that is soft, white, fleshy, sweet and sour. It is a relative of the cherimoya.

soymilk: A nutritious milk made by soaking, crushing, boiling, and straining soybeans. Soymilk contains equivalent protein content and has properties similar to cow's milk. Soymilk can be purchased already prepared at health food, international, and Asian food stores and some supermarkets. It is available in several flavors. There are also low-fat varieties.

squash blossoms: The large blossoms of summer squash plants. They are a seasonal delicacy and should be picked early in the morning while they are still open.

star fruit (carambula): A wonderful, golden tropical fruit with a slight citrus flavor. Their unique shape and bright color make them a perfect choice for fruit salads or garnishes.
substitute: passion fruit

sugar apple: Another relative of the cherimoya, sugar apples are a wonderful tropical fruit with a very sweet taste and a soft, fleshy texture.
substitute: very ripe, sweet apricots or plums

tamarind: These tart, citric, tropical pods from the tamarind tree have been used in India for many centuries. It is often sold in Mexican food stores as a thick prepared concentrate for drinks. The tamarind tree can live for over 100 years.
substitute: dates or sour cherries

tania: A small fibrous tuber that is grown in tropical regions. It is used throughout the Caribbean. They can be cooked like sweet potatoes.
substitute: white yams, dasheen, or white potatoes

tempeh: A cultured food, like yogurt, usually made from soybeans but also made from other beans and grains. Tempeh has been a staple source of protein in Indonesia for several hundred years. It has a chewy texture, and can be baked, barbecued, steamed, or fried. Tempeh can be purchased in health food stores or made at home.

toasted soy flour: Toasted soy flour is made by first roasting the soybeans and then grinding them into a fine flour. It has a nuttier flavor than fresh soy flour.

tofu: A mild-tasting, protein rich food made from curdled soymilk. Tofu has the appearance of a white dairy cheese but has a softer texture. Tofu is extremely versatile because it absorbs flavors easily.

tokara: A tofu-like food made from soymilk and okara that are curdled together and then pressed. This is good way to make use of some of the okara that is left after making soymilk or tofu.
substitute: tofu

tortas: Small fry cakes usually made with corn masa, baking powder, and seasonings

tortilla: Corn or wheat dough rolled out into a flat circular shape and then cooked on both sides in a dry skillet. A staple food in Latin American, tortillas can be served alone, with other foods, or filled and rolled as a burrito.

turmeric: An East Indian plant and member of the ginger family. The powdered roots are used for seasoning and yellow coloring.

yam: A large white or yellow fleshed tuber that is a staple of all tropical regions. Yams are not the same as North American yams or sweet potatoes.
substitute: sweet potatoes

yucca (see cassava): Also known as manioc, yucca is the Central American name for the cassava plant.

Recipe Notes

Flours

We have distinguished each of the flours (wheat, full fat soy and toasted soy, cassava, rice etc.) contained in this cookbook because they have distinctly different traits. Unbleached white flour is lighter and milder tasting than whole wheat flour, and is the flour recommended in many of these recipes. Of course, whole wheat flour can be used if desired. Because of its high oil content, full-fat soy flour should be refrigerated to keep it from going rancid.

Tofu

Packaged tofu is usually labeled extra firm, firm, regular, or soft. For the tofu recipes in this cookbook, except those calling for blended tofu, we recommend you use a firm or extra firm tofu. If the tofu where you shop is not labeled, ask your grocer what kind it is.

Grating tofu and tempeh

Firm tofu and tempeh can be grated to a very nice consistency. We have found that grated tofu and tempeh blend into most of these recipes better than when crumbled. Before attempting to grate tofu we recommend that you gently squeeze the extra water out of the tofu by hand without breaking it apart. Grate slowly and do not press down on the grater as hard as you would when grating vegetables or dairy cheese.

Replacing okara with grated tofu or tempeh

Many of the recipes we have adapted for this cookbook are made in their countries of origin using a milky fiber residue ("okara" in North America, "payana" in Nicaragua, or "parche" in the Caribbean) remaining from the process of making soymilk or tofu. Okara contains approximately 5% protein as well as fiber, vitamins, and minerals. Because people in North America generally do not make milk and tofu at home, we have replaced the okara needed in most of the recipes with grated tofu or tempeh. For best results be sure to squeeze excess water out of the grated tofu or tempeh before using them in any of the okara recipes.

Cooking, breaking, and dehulling soybeans

Whole soybeans must be cooked for many hours to be fully cooked and be easily digested. Soybeans may be pressure cooked for 1 hour. Carefully follow the instructions that come with your pressure cooker. If you pressure cook soybeans, they must be closely watched while cooking. The hulls of soybeans tend to separate and may clog the steam vent on a pressure cooker which may cause the pressure safety valve to blow out. If the release valve becomes quiet while cooking, immediately remove the pressure cooker from the heat. Allow the pressure cooker to cool and the pressure to come down. Carefully open the lid, and remove any hulls that are blocking the opening or are floating on top, and continue cooking. When done, the soybeans should be soft enough to crush against the roof of your mouth with your tongue. To cut down on cooking time, many soybean recipes that have been developed throughout the world use broken soybeans. To break whole soybeans you do not need elaborate equipment. You can use a grain or coffee mill, grinding stone, or large mortar and pestle. Clean, dry beans should be used. After breaking the soybeans into about eight pieces each, remove the hulls by winnowing (gently tossing them in a bowl or colander in the open air), or place the broken soybeans in water, stir, and scoop off the hulls that float to the top.

Hand mills and blenders

Some of the recipes call for using an electric or hand powered grain or coffee mill for grinding roasted soybeans, corn meal, dry hot peppers, whole cloves, and other ingredients into a meal or flour consistency. Some blenders and food processors can be used instead of mills, however, we recommend that you read the instructions that came with your blender or food processor before attempting to mill toasted soybeans, rice, or other hard ingredients. Also, when blending tofu and tempeh with other ingredients, we recommend that you stir all the required ingredients together first, and then blend them with the tofu or tempeh one cup at a time. Sometimes, when using a blender, you may have to add a little more water than is called for in a recipe.

North America

The American diet utilizes the highest per capita amount of animal products in the world. Yet substitutes for meat and dairy items can be easily incorporated into a traditional American diet, with no loss of taste, and with an increase in good nutrition.

We hope you will enjoy the recipes included in this section, which represent a combination of some of our own families' American favorites and some adaptations of traditional southwest Native American cuisine.

The Bronx

In the spring of 1977, the South Bronx in New York City resembled Dresden at the end of World War II. Hulking, abandoned tenements were being burned for the insurance or stripped of their radiators, windows, banisters, or anything else of value. President Jimmy Carter visited the Bronx and declared it a disaster area. At one point it got so bad that the Emergency Medical Services of the city were unwilling to go into the South Bronx after dark. Plenty was invited by a group of local community activists to provide some emergency back up. We sent a group of our Plenty medical volunteers—EMTs (emergency medical technicians), paramedics, and a midwife, along with their families, and a fully refurbished ambulance. They shoveled the broken glass and rubbish out of an empty tenement, cleaned it up, and established the Bronx Plenty Ambulance Service, licensed by the State of New York and free to all residents. Besides providing emergency transport, over many years these volunteers also trained thousands of people in CPR and first aid and graduated more than two hundred EMTs and paramedics.

In their spare time, Plenty Ambulance Service volunteers assisted at many health fairs where they took blood pressures, did health screening, and nutrition education. At these fairs they offered free soybean burritos as an introduction to soy foods. They were very popular, and there were always long lines of people waiting to be served.

Carol Nelson—RN, midwife

Native Americans

Plenty began working with the Oglala Lakota people at Pine Ridge Reservation in South Dakota in 1981 and has been supporting reforestation, health care, crafts marketing, and agricultural projects since then. A community garden project aimed at helping families grow and market organic vegetables and fruits now involves more than 200 families on the reservation.

A similar project is underway to improve the economic, and agricultural opportunities for the 1,000 Wailaki and Nomlaki people living at the Round Valley reservation near Covelo in northern California.

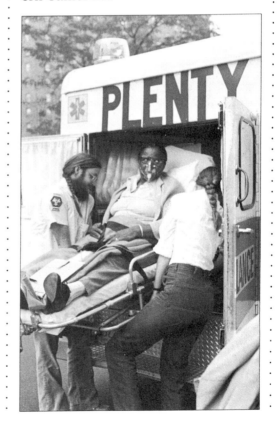

Main Dishes

Pumpkin and Tofu

To help keep your family warm and healthy when autumn winds turn cold.

**1 small pumpkin, peeled, seeded, and
    cut into small chunks**
½ lb firm tofu, cubed
1 tablespoon oil
1 small hot pepper, diced
1 small onion, chopped
2 teaspoons salt
½ cup water

In a medium saucepan, steam or boil the pumpkin until soft. In a medium frying pan, brown the tofu on all sides in hot oil. Add the hot pepper, onion, salt, and water to the tofu, and cook for 3 to 5 minutes. Serve the seasoned tofu alongside the pumpkin, and top with a little margarine and salt.

Serves 4

Per serving: Calories: 121, Protein: 5 gm., Fat: 5 gm., Carbohydrates: 11 gm.

Squash Blossom Stew

These balanced subtle flavors provide a pleasing meal for the whole family. This a wonderful dish that you can make when you have squash in your garden.

10 squash blossoms (page 14)
4 cups dry corn
½ lb tofu, cut in small cubes
salt to taste

Cut the squash blossoms in the early morning when they are open and before the squash begins to mature. Rinse the blossoms, then steam or gently boil them in a large saucepan until very tender, about 5 minutes. Drain the water and mash the blossoms. Place the corn in a large pot with enough water to cover the kernels and boil until soft, about 40 minutes. Add the tofu, mashed squash blossoms, and salt to taste, and simmer for another 10 to 15 minutes. Serve hot with your favorite breads or crackers.

Serves 4 to 6

Per serving: Calories: 142, Protein: 6 gm., Fat: 2 gm., Carbohydrates: 25 gm.

Tofu Pot Pie

This is an excellent meal when you want something home cooked that is hot and filling.

Pastry Crust:
1 cup whole wheat flour
½ teaspoon salt
3 tablespoons oil
2 to 3 tablespoons water

Pie Filling:
¼ cup unbleached white flour
1 tablespoon nutritional yeast flakes
1 teaspoon salt
½ teaspoon garlic powder
2 cups tofu, cut into ½-inch cubes
2 tablespoons oil
1 cup onions, chopped
½ cup celery, sliced
1 carrot, chopped
1 cup whole kernel corn
1 cup green peas
2 tablespoons nutritional yeast

To make the pastry crust:
Mix the flour and salt, then add the oil and enough water to form a ball. Roll out between two sheets of waxed paper.
To make the filling:
Preheat the oven to 375°F. Combine the flour, 1 tablespoon nutritional yeast, salt, and garlic powder in a small bowl. Add the tofu and stir to coat all of the cubes. Heat the oil in a medium skillet, and sauté the breaded tofu until lightly browned, then add the onions and celery. When they are soft, add the carrots, corn, and peas, and simmer until the carrots are soft, adding a little water if needed. Stir in 2 tablespoons nutritional yeast with the vegetables. Place the filling in a medium casserole dish lined with the pastry crust. Bake for 30 to 40 minutes until the top is slightly browned.

Serves 4 to 6

Per serving: Calories: 382, Protein: 15 gm., Fat: 17 gm., Carbohydrates: 39 gm.

Squash Blossoms with Corn Meal and Tofu

A seasonal taste treat.

**10 to 12 large squash blossoms
(page 14)**
⅔ cup corn meal
⅓ cup tofu, crumbled
½ teaspoon salt
3 tablespoon margarine, melted
½ cup water

Squash blossoms should be cut in the early morning when they are open. Preheat the oven to 350°F. Gently rinse the blossoms. Mix the corn meal, tofu, salt, and margarine together in a medium bowl. Slowly stir in the water to make a thick batter. Fill each blossom with a small amount of the corn-tofu batter, and fold the petals in over the top of the filling. Place the blossoms upright in a well oiled baking pan, and bake for about 20 minutes. Serve a hot bowl of chili with this delicious side dish.

Serves 4 to 6

Per serving: Calories: 139, Protein: 3 gm., Fat: 7 gm., Carbohydrates: 15 gm.

Tempeh Cacciatore

For those who think that eating meals without meat is uninspiring.

½ lb of tempeh
½ cup flour
½ teaspoon salt
½ teaspoon black pepper
¼ cup oil
1 cup onions, chopped
4 cups tomato sauce
⅛ teaspoon sweet marjoram
⅛ teaspoon thyme
2 cloves garlic, minced
1 bay leaf
1 teaspoon salt
1 teaspoon basil
1 teaspoon oregano

Cut the tempeh into 12 thin slices. Mix the flour, salt, and pepper together in a small bowl. Coat each strip of tempeh with the mixture, and fry in a medium skillet with hot oil and the onions until the tempeh is golden brown on both sides. Add the tomato sauce and all remaining seasonings. Simmer on low heat for one hour. Serve with salad and garlic bread.

Serves 6

Per serving: Calories: 247, Protein: 9 gm., Fat: 12 gm., Carbohydrates: 26 gm.

Eggplant Parmesan

1 medium eggplant
1 teaspoon salt
1 cup unbleached white flour
¼ cup oil
1 cup tomato sauce
½ cup tofu, grated
1 cup mozzarella cheese, grated

Slice the eggplant into rounds 1/2 inch thick, place in a large bowl with salted water, and weigh down. Let set for 30 minutes, and drain. Dredge each slice with flour, and fry in hot oil until browned on both sides. Place on a baking sheet one layer thick, and top the slices with the tomato sauce, a thin layer of grated tofu, and cheese. Broil until the sauce bubbles and browns. Serve hot with garlic bread and a garden salad.

Serves 4

Per serving: Calories: 433, Protein: 14 gm., Fat: 23 gm., Carbohydrates: 40 gm.

Tempeh Sausage Patties

Breakfast doesn't come early enough for children waiting to feast on these patties.

½ lb tempeh
½ teaspoon sage
½ teaspoon marjoram
½ teaspoon thyme
½ teaspoon cumin
2 tablespoons unbleached white flour
2 tablespoons warm water
1 tablespoon oil
2 tablespoons soy sauce

Steam the tempeh for 20 minutes, cool, and grate. In a medium bowl, mix the tempeh, sage, marjoram, thyme, cumin, flour, water, 2 teaspoons oil, and soy sauce. Mix and press firmly into patties. In a large skillet, fry the patties in 1 teaspoon of oil until browned on both sides. Serve with your favorite biscuits or bread, fruit, and a cup of tea for a great breakfast send off.

Serves 4

Per serving: Calories: 162, Protein: 11 gm., Fat: 7 gm., Carbohydrates: 13 gm.

Salad

Pineapple Shells with Fruit Salad

A summer fruit salad with something extra! Served with meals or alone, this fruit salad tastes great anytime.

½ **lb tempeh, sliced in half**
½ **cup water**
¾ **cup apple juice**
2 tablespoons tamari
2 tablespoons mirin
½ **teaspoon fresh gingerroot, grated**
1 fresh ripe pineapple
2 fresh peaches
1 cup fresh strawberries
1 cup blueberries or seedless grapes
2 tablespoons lemon juice

In a medium saucepan, simmer the tempeh for 20 minutes in the water and ½ cup of apple juice. Cool the tempeh, cut it into small cubes, and toss with a marinade of the remaining apple juice, tamari, mirin, and ginger. Cover the tempeh and chill for several hours or overnight. Slice the pineapple in half lengthwise, remove the flesh from the pineapple, and remove the center core. Save the pineapple shell. Cut the meat of the pineapple into chunks, cover, and chill. Dip the peaches into boiling water for 30 seconds, place in cold water, remove the peel, and slice. In a large bowl, mix the pineapple chunks, sliced peaches, strawberries, and blueberries or grapes. Stir in the marinated tempeh and lemon juice, and spoon the mixture into the pineapple shells.

Serves 6

Per serving: Calories: 180, Protein: 8 gm., Fat: 3 gm., Carbohydrates: 30 gm.

Breads

Corn-Soy Fry Bread

When this traditional Native American staple is fortified with corn and soy, it adds more protein and a nuttier flavor.

3 cups unbleached white flour
⅓ cup full-fat soy flour
⅓ cup corn meal
5 teaspoons baking powder
1 teaspoon salt
2 cups water
oil for frying

Mix the flours, corn meal, baking powder, and salt in large bowl. Gradually stir in the water to make a soft dough. Cover and let set for 30 minutes. Shape the dough into 2-inch balls, and roll them out on a floured board into circles about ⅛ inch thick. Heat a generous amount of oil in a deep frying pan. When the oil is very hot, about 360°F, fry the dough until brown on both sides. Drain on paper towels. Serve with flavored and stewed beans, tofu, or tempeh.

Serves 6

Per serving: Calories: 255, Protein: 9 gm., Fat: 1 gm., Carbohydrates: 51 gm.

Pinole Soy Bread

This bread is a meal in itself.

⅔ cup unbleached white flour
⅓ cup soy flour
¾ cup pinole (page 13)
½ teaspoon baking powder
2 tablespoons margarine
1½ cups creamed corn
½ cup soymilk
4 to 5 green chili peppers, finely
    chopped
1 cup cheddar cheese, grated

Preheat the oven to 350°F. In a large bowl, stir together the flours, pinole, and baking powder. Melt the margarine and add it to the flour with the creamed corn and soymilk. Spoon half of the batter into a greased 8 x 9-inch baking pan. Sprinkle with ½ of the grated cheese, the chilies, and the remaining cheese. Top with the remaining batter, and bake for 1 hour. Let cool 15 minutes, then cut into squares.

Serves 8

Per serving: Calories: 227, Protein: 9 gm., Fat: 9 gm., Carbohydrates: 28 gm.

Desserts

Oatmeal Cookies

The tried and true number one favorite snack of kids and adults.

½ **cup margarine**
⅓ **cup oil**
½ **cup brown sugar**
½ **cup white sugar**
⅓ **cup soymilk**
2 **teaspoons vanilla**
2½ **cups unbleached white flour**
1 **teaspoon baking powder**
1 **teaspoon baking soda**
¼ **teaspoon salt**
3 **cups rolled oats**
½ **cup raisins**

Preheat the oven to 350°F. In a large bowl, cream the margarine and oil together, then cream in the sugars. Add the soymilk and vanilla. Beat in the flour, baking powder, baking soda, and salt. Add the oats and raisins, and mix well. Place tablespoonfuls of the dough on oiled cookie sheets. Bake for about 15 minutes or until the undersides just start turning brown. Enjoy with soymilk, coffee, or tea.

Makes 12 to 18 cookies

Per Cookie: Calories: 285, Protein: 5 gm., Fat: 11 gm., Carbohydrates: 40 gm.

Pinole Pudding

A sweet treat common to Native American tribes of the southwest.

⅓ **cup sugar**
¼ **cup cornstarch**
3 **tablespoons pinole (page 13)**
2 **cups soymilk**
½ **cup tofu, blended**
2 **tablespoons margarine**
1 **teaspoon vanilla**

Mix the sugar, cornstarch, and pinole in a medium saucepan. Gradually add the soymilk and tofu. Cook on medium heat, stirring constantly, until the mixture boils. Boil for 1 minute, remove from the heat, stir in the margarine and vanilla, and chill. Serve alone, as a snack, or as dessert.

Serves 4

Per serving: Calories: 225, Protein: 6 gm., Fat: 8 gm., Carbohydrates: 30 gm.

Tofu Pinole Bars

1 cup margarine
1 cup sugar
1 cup tofu, grated
1 cup pinole (page 13)
1 cup unbleached white flour

Preheat the oven to 375°F. In a medium bowl, cream together the margarine and sugar . Beat in the tofu and pinole. Stir in the flour just until mixed. Spread in a greased 9" x 13" baking pan. Bake for 15 to 20 minutes. Cut into bars.

Makes 14 bars

Per bar: Calories: 245, Protein: 3 gm., Fat: 13 gm., Carbohydrates: 27 gm.

The Caribbean

The Caribbean Sea contains more than 1,000 islands, comprising 24 countries, which share numerous commercial, educational, judicial, and protectorate agreements, and treaties.

In the Caribbean islands, soy foods continue to gain in popularity. Soy businesses in Jamaica that were only supplying tofu to five small health food stores five years ago are now supplying more than fifty Jamaican stores and restaurants with tofu, soy ice cream, cereals, snack foods, soymilk, and other soy products. From Dominica, tofu, soybean cereals, and snack foods have been sold and distributed to the neighboring islands of Guadeloupe, Martinique, Barbados, and Antigua. Visitors to St. Lucia and St. Vincent can also find small restaurants and health food stores serving a variety of fresh and packaged soybean and vegetarian products.

From the Jamaican favorite, roots pumpkin roti, to the calalou soups and passion fruit puddings of the lower Antilles, soy foods are a welcome addition to the delicious traditional dishes enjoyed by residents and visitors throughout the Caribbean. In this section, you can discover and enjoy delectable island cuisine without leaving home.

Plenty representatives made their first voyage to the Caribbean in 1983 aboard a 90 foot sailing ship, after receiving requests for technical and material assistance from leaders of the Carib people living on the Eastern Caribbean island of Dominica. The Dominican Caribs are the last indigenous people within the Caribbean islands who continue to own and manage their land in common trust. Since 1983, Plenty has supported many small community projects within the Carib Territory including installation of solar electricity at a primary school, construction of a council office/community building, a mechanics workshop, and a food processing kitchen. In addition, Plenty has provided technical and material support to a number of groups who have been learning to grow, process, and market soybean products in Dominica, St. Vincent, St. Lucia, and Jamaica.

The Story of Ruby Charles

Born and raised in Dominica and already a vegetarian, I started working with Plenty Canada in 1985 as Co-Director of programs. I became involved in all aspects of the work, especially the processing and preparation of soy foods. It was quite an experience working with soy and really a delight creating new recipes. We were very concerned about taste, knowing that people would reject unfamiliar foods. But, by using local seasonings, we were able to create soy dishes which were quite similar to the traditional meat-and-fish-based diet.

After learning to cook with soy, I was ready to teach others. We organized soy cooking demonstrations island-wide. By then, soy had become somewhat of a revolution in Dominica. The demonstration classes enabled me to reach people from all walks of life—nurses, doctors, school teachers, housewives, farmers, school children, civil servants, and small business people. We shared cooking skills and nutrition education ideas and learned a lot from each other.

The excitement and suspense would begin when we all gathered together to milk the bean. Some would be grinding the beans, chopping seasonings and vegetables, stirring, mixing, or tasting while others just watched and waited in anticipation. I always enjoyed the look on people's faces when they would taste the soymilk or tofu for the first time. I would hold my breath hoping that they would not be disappointed. Then I would be greeted with sudden bursts of surprised expressions and disbelief. They would say, "I can't believe this is made out of soybean!"—"This one tastes like fish."—"Wait 'til we tell the rest of the family, they won't believe what this is made from." Sometimes I would hardly get more than a taste from the cooking as the participants would all be busy filling containers to take home.

Ruby Charles

Main Dishes

Ginger Curried Tofu Cabbage

½ lb firm tofu, cut into small cubes
¼ cup soy sauce
1 teaspoon curry powder
1 teaspoon salt
1 clove garlic, crushed
1 tablespoon oil
1 small cabbage
2 cups celery, chopped
1 small onion, chopped
1 sprig fresh parsley, diced
1 teaspoon fresh gingerroot, crushed

Marinate the tofu in the soy sauce, curry, salt, and garlic. In a large frying pan, sauté the tofu in the oil until golden brown. Wash and cut the cabbage in big slices. Add the cabbage, celery, onion, parsley, and ginger and cook for 5 minutes, stirring frequently. Serve with white potatoes, tania, dasheen, bread fruit, or yams.

Serves 4 to 6

Per serving: Calories: 96, Protein: 6 gm., Fat: 5 gm., Carbohydrates: 7 gm.

Pumpkin, Tofu, and Rice

Pumpkins in the Caribbean are similar to winter squash in North America.

1 lb rice
1 lb firm tofu
¼ cup soy sauce
3 cloves garlic, minced
2 tablespoon oil
½ lb pumpkin (or winter squash), grated
1 stem celery, chopped
1 sprig fresh parsley, minced

Cook the rice and let it cool. Cut the tofu into small cubes, and season with soy sauce and garlic. Heat the oil, add the seasoned tofu, and stir fry until golden brown. Remove the tofu from the pan. In the same pan, sauté the pumpkin and celery in the same seasonings until soft, adding a little water if necessary. Add cooked rice and mix well. Add the tofu and stir fry for 5 minutes. Serve hot with your favorite green salad.

Serves 6

Per serving: Calories: 208, Protein: 9 gm., Fat: 8 gm., Carbohydrates: 24 gm.

Breadfruit and Tofu Souce

Not a misspelling, "souce" is pronounced "soose." This dish has a creamy mild flavor that goes well with steamed garden vegetables.

½ breadfruit (page 10)
    or 2 medium white potatoes
1 stalk green onion, diced
1 medium onion, chopped
juice of ½ lime
1 clove garlic, crushed
1 teaspoon pepper
1 teaspoon salt
2 cups water
½ lb firm tofu, diced

Wash the breadfruit, cut into 3 large pieces, boil until soft, and remove the skin. Drain and cut into small pieces. Prepare the sauce by mixing the green onion, onion, lime juice, garlic, pepper, salt, and water. Add the breadfruit and tofu to the sauce, mix well, cook for 3 minutes. This meal can be served hot or cold. You can also use two large white potatoes, green bananas, yams, or bread nuts instead of the breadfruit.

Serves 4

Per serving: Calories: 148, Protein: 6 gm., Fat: 3 gm., Carbohydrates: 25 gm.

Dominica Style Tomato Tofu Casserole

2 lbs firm tofu, grated
2 medium tomatoes, chopped
½ cup tomato sauce
2 tablespoons fresh parsley
1 teaspoon fresh gingerroot, crushed
1 teaspoon black pepper
¼ teaspoon salt
¼ lb cheddar cheese, grated

Preheat the oven to 350°F. Mix together the tofu, tomatoes, tomato sauce, parsley, ginger, pepper, and salt. Spread in an oiled, medium baking pan, cover with the cheese, and bake for 20 minutes.

Serves 4 to 6

Per serving: Calories: 246, Protein: 19 gm., Fat: 15 gm., Carbohydrates: 7 gm.

Mini Breadfruit Pie

The Caribbean version of pot pies.

1 lb breadfruit (page 10) or 2 medium white potatoes, chopped, cooked, and peeled
5 tablespoons unbleached white flour
1 teaspoon oil
2 ripe tomatoes, chopped
1 onion, chopped
1 stalk celery, diced
2 tablespoons soy sauce
1 sprig fresh parsley, diced
3 cloves garlic, crushed
1 tablespoon oil
1 lb firm tofu, diced

Mash the breadfruit, making sure that there are no lumps. Add the flour and 1 teaspoon oil, knead well, and shape into smooth balls about 2 inches in diameter. Place them in an oiled dish, and cover. Preheat the oven to 350°F. In a medium saucepan, sauté the tomatoes, onion, celery, soy sauce, parsley, and garlic in 1 tablespoon oil until tender. Add the tofu and cook for 5 minutes, stirring frequently. Roll out the breadfruit dough until it is ¼ inch thick. Fill with the tofu and tomato mixture, fold over, and seal the edges. Place in an oiled and floured baking pan, and bake for 10 to 15 minutes.

Makes 8 pies

Per pie: Calories: 176, Protein: 6 gm., Fat: 9 gm., Carbohydrates: 16 gm.

Dasheen Casserole

Dasheen has a distinctive, mild flavor and chewy texture that makes it a delight to eat.

1 large dasheen (page 11) or 3 white potatoes, peeled and cubed
1½ lbs tofu, mashed
⅔ cup onions, chopped
½ carrot, grated
¼ teaspoon granulated garlic
¼ cup fresh parsley, chopped
1¼ teaspoons salt
1 teaspoon soy sauce
1 tablespoon oil

Steam the dasheen or potatoes until tender, drain, and mash. Preheat the oven to 350°F. Sauté the tofu, onions, carrot, and seasonings in the oil for 10 minutes. Mix with the dasheen or potatoes. Place in an lightly oiled, medium baking dish, and bake for 35 minutes.

Serves 6

Per serving: Calories: 173, Protein: 9 gm., Fat: 7 gm., Carbohydrates: 18 gm.

Parrots Peleau

This is a meal unto itself.

½ lb soybeans
½ lb tempeh or firm tofu
½ cup soy sauce
10 cloves garlic
3 sprigs fresh thyme or 1 teaspoon dried
    thyme
3 cups water
1 lb rice
2 onions, chopped
3 carrots, diced
¼ small cabbage, chopped
4 stalks celery, diced
1 tablespoon oil
½ cup soymilk
¼ cup tomato paste
2 tomatoes, diced
3 large sweet peppers, chopped

Pressure cook the soybeans until soft, about 1 hour. Slice and marinate the tempeh or tofu in ¼ cup soy sauce, 1 clove garlic, minced, and 1 sprig of thyme. Boil the water with 2 cloves of garlic. Wash the rice and add to the boiling water. Cook for 5 minutes, then add the onions, carrots, cabbage, celery, and salt. In another pot sauté the tofu or tempeh for 10 minutes in the oil. When the rice is almost done, add the cooked soybeans, tempeh or tofu, ¼ cup soy sauce, the rest of the thyme and garlic, soymilk, tomato paste, tomatoes, and sweet peppers. Mix everything well and cook on low heat until the rice is done.

Serves 8

Per serving: Calories: 254, Protein: 13 gm., Fat: 7 gm., Carbohydrates: 34 gm.

Savory Tokara Pie

Per serving: Calories: 251, Protein: 12 gm., Fat: 7 gm., Carbohydrates: 34 gm.

1 teaspoon baking yeast
½ cup warm water
2 cups whole wheat flour
1 tablespoon oil
1 teaspoon salt
2 medium tomatoes
3 stalks celery, chopped
1 medium onion, chopped
4 cloves garlic, crushed
3 tablespoons soy sauce
1 tablespoon dry thyme
1 teaspoon oil
1 lb tofu or tokara (page 14), grated
1 tablespoon lime juice
1 tablespoon nutritional yeast

In a small bowl, combine the baking yeast with ½ cup warm water and let set until foamy. In a medium bowl, whisk together the yeast mixture, flour, 1 tablespoon oil, and salt, and mix well. Knead the dough, roll into a smooth ball, and let rise. Preheat the oven to 350°F. Sauté the tomatoes, celery, onion, garlic, soy sauce, and thyme in 1 teaspoon oil for 3 to 5 minutes. Add the tofu or tokara, mix well, and stir fry for 10 minutes. Add the lime juice and nutritional yeast to taste. Roll out the dough in a circle ⅛ inch thick, and spread the vegetable filling in a thin layer over the dough. Fold over into a half circle, seal the edges, place on a cookie sheet, and bake for 20 minutes.

Serves 4 to 6

Islander Balls and Gravy

1 cup tofu or tokara, grated
½ cup flour
2 carrots, grated
½ onion, chopped
¼ cup fine bread crumbs
¼ cup soy sauce
1 teaspoon black pepper
½ teaspoon salt
1 clove garlic, minced
¼ cup corn meal
oil for frying

Combine the tofu or tokara, ¼ cup flour, carrots, onion, bread crumbs, soy sauce, black pepper, salt, and garlic, and shape into balls. In a bowl, mix the flour and corn meal. Coat the balls with the remaining flour mixture, and fry until golden brown.

Gravy:
½ cup coconut milk
1 cup water
¼ cup ketchup
2 stalks green onions, chopped
2 cloves garlic, minced
4 tablespoons soy sauce
2 tablespoons corn starch
2 tablespoons sugar
1 teaspoon black pepper
1 teaspoon dry thyme
1 teaspoon powdered ginger

Whisk all of the ingredients together in a saucepan, and simmer until thick, adding salt to taste. Add the tokara balls to the gravy, and simmer for 2 minutes. Serve hot over rice.

Serves 4

Per serving: Calories: 320, Protein: 11 gm., Fat: 10 gm., Carbohydrates: 45 gm.

Potato Pie

1 lb white potatoes, cubed
1 lb tofu or tokara (page 14), mashed
1 large onion, chopped
1 bell pepper, chopped
3 cloves garlic, minced
2 sprigs fresh parsley, minced
1 teaspoon dry thyme
3 tablespoons soy sauce
2 teaspoons lime juice
1½ teaspoons salt
1 teaspoon black pepper
2 teaspoons oil

Cook and mash the potatoes. Sauté the tofu or tokara with all of the other ingredients, except the potatoes, in the oil. Preheat the oven to 350°F. In a lightly oiled, medium baking dish, place 1 thin layer of mashed potatoes. Add 1 layer of tofu/vegetable mixture. Alternate layers until all ingredients are used, and top with mashed potatoes. Bake 25 to 30 minutes or until the top is brown.

Serves 6

Per serving: Calories: 159, Protein: 8 gm., Fat: 5 gm., Carbohydrates: 20 gm.

Roots Pumpkin Roti

1 lb firm tofu, cubed
2 medium onions, chopped
3 cloves garlic, crushed
1 stalk celery, minced
1 sprig fresh parsley, minced
1 sprig fresh thyme leaves
2 tablespoons curry powder
½ teaspoon black pepper
2 tablespoons oil
1¼ lbs pumpkin or squash, cubed
1 lb potatoes, cubed
1 cup water

Dough :
3 cups unbleached white flour
¼ teaspoon salt (optional)
1 tablespoon oil
1 cup water

Sauté the tofu, onions, garlic, celery, parsley, thyme, curry, and pepper in the oil. Add the pumpkin and potatoes, and sauté for 5 more minutes. Add 1 cup water and simmer until the potato and pumpkin are cooked. To make the dough, mix together the flour and salt. Make a hole in the middle, and add the oil and water, mixing until a firm ball is formed. Knead just long enough for a smooth dough to develop. Break into 8 equal balls, and roll out into thin 6-inch circles. Heat both sides on a dry, floured skillet until they are cooked but still soft and flexible. Fill with the roti mix, fold in half, fold the ends to prevent spilling, and serve.

Serves 8

Per serving: Calories: 320, Protein: 10 gm., Fat: 8 gm., Carbohydrates: 52 gm.

West Indies Pizza

A traditional favorite with a tropical twist!

1 (10 to 12-inch) pizza crust

Sauce :
14 ounces tomato sauce
1 tablespoon thyme
1 tablespoon soy sauce
1 teaspoon salt
⅔ cup fresh parsley, chopped
1 teaspoon pepper sauce
3 cloves garlic, minced

Topping :
¼ lb firm tofu, grated
¼ lb mozzarella cheese, grated
½ medium tomato, diced
1 small onion, diced
1 stalk green onion, diced
2 stalks celery, diced
1 tablespoon black pepper
1½ cups pineapple, cubed

Make or buy a 10 to 12-inch pizza dough. Preheat the oven to 375°F. Lay the dough on a pizza pan. Mix the sauce ingredients, and spread on the pizza dough. Spread the tofu, cheese, tomato, onions, celery, and black pepper over the sauce, and top with the pineapple. Bake for about 25 minutes or until the cheese begins to bubble.

Makes 8 slices

Per slice: Calories: 192, Protein: 8 gm., Fat: 4 gm., Carbohydrates: 30 gm.

Bryan's Soybean Hash

1 lb cooked soybeans (4 cups)
1 cup soymilk
2 cloves garlic, crushed
6 green onions, minced
4 stalks of celery, minced
4 carrots, grated
1 large bell pepper, chopped
2 tablespoons nutritional yeast
2 tablespoons soy sauce
¾ lb reduced-fat cheddar cheese, grated
1 lb potatoes, cubed
1 teaspoon salt

Grind the soybeans in a hand mill or blender, adding a little of the soymilk with the vegetables and nutritional yeast. Add the soy sauce and cheese, and blend well. Preheat the oven to 350°F. Boil and mash the potatoes with the salt and the remaining soymilk. Combine the soybeans and potatoes, and mix well. Bake in a greased, medium baking dish for 30 minutes.

Serves 10

Per serving: Calories: 263, Protein: 18 gm., Fat: 10 gm., Carbohydrates: 21 gm.

Caribbean Baked Tempeh

½ lb tempeh, cut in small cubes
1½ teaspoons oil
½ cup water
1 small onion, chopped
1 teaspoon fresh gingerroot, grated
1 teaspoon cumin
juice of 1 lemon
3 tablespoons tomato paste
½ cup cheese, grated (optional)

Sauté the tempeh in the oil until golden brown. Add the water, cover, and steam for 4 minutes. Preheat the oven to 350°F. Push the tempeh to the side of the pan, add the onion, and cook until the onion is soft. Add the ginger, cumin, lemon juice, and tomato paste, and simmer for 10 minutes. Pour into a greased baking pan, top with cheese, and bake for 20 minutes.

Serves 4

Per serving: Calories: 151, Protein: 10 gm., Fat: 5 gm., Carbohydrates: 15 gm.

Creole Gumbo

½ lb tempeh, cut in small cubes
¾ cup soy sauce
1 tablespoon lime juice
2 cloves garlic, minced
1 tablespoon oil
2 cups fresh okra, sliced in rounds
2 small onions, chopped
2 medium tomatoes, chopped
1 medium green pepper, chopped
2 stalks celery, diced
1 teaspoon dry thyme
½ teaspoon salt
1 teaspoon oil

Steam the tempeh for 10 minutes, and drain. Marinate the tempeh in the soy sauce, lime juice, and garlic for 30 minutes. Remove the tempeh from marinade, and stir fry in 1 tablespoon oil until brown. Remove the tempeh from the pan. In the same pan, sauté the vegetables and all seasonings in 1 teaspoon oil. Add a little water and cook until the onions are limp. Add the remaining marinade and simmer for 20 minutes. Add the tempeh and cook for 5 more minutes.

Serves 6

Per serving: Calories: 158, Protein: 11 gm., Fat: 6 gm., Carbohydrates: 15 gm.

Saucy Tempeh Turnover

- 1 lb tempeh
- ¼ cup soy sauce
- ¼ cup water
- 1 tablespoon powdered garlic
- 1 tablespoon nutritional yeast
- 1 tablespoon sugar
- 1 cup water
- 1½ teaspoons baking yeast
- 2 cups unbleached white flour
- 1 cup whole wheat flour
- 1 tablespoon oil (for dough)
- oil for frying tempeh
- 1 cup onions, diced
- 1 teaspoon oil
- 2 tablespoons ketchup
- 1 tablespoon wet mustard
- 1 cup tomato sauce
- 1 tablespoon coriander powder
- 1 teaspoon sugar
- 1 teaspoon salt

Cut the tempeh into thin slices, and marinate in the soy sauce, ¼ cup water, garlic, and nutritional yeast for at least 1 hour or overnight in the refrigerator. Dissolve the sugar in 1 cup lukewarm water. Sprinkle in the baking yeast and 1 cup of flour, mix well, and let stand for 10 minutes. Add the oil and enough white and whole wheat flours to knead into a smooth dough. Cover and let rise in a warm place. While the dough is rising, fry the tempeh slices in hot oil but not too crisp. Sauté the onions in 1 teaspoon oil with the ketchup, mustard, tomato sauce, coriander, sugar, and salt until the onions are tender. Preheat the oven to 350°F. Roll out the dough on a floured board ⅛ to ¼ inch thick. Place the tempeh slices on one half of the rolled dough, and cover with the sauce and onions. Fold the dough, press the edges together, and bake for 25 minutes.

Makes 12 pieces

Per piece: Calories: 214, Protein: 11 gm., Fat: 5 gm., Carbohydrates: 33 gm.

Tempeh Goulash

2 medium onions, chopped
2 stalks celery, chopped
2 tablespoons oil
½ lb tempeh, cut in small cubes
¾ cup water
1 cup ketchup
2 small green peppers, chopped
¼ cup soy sauce
1 teaspoon garlic, minced
1 teaspoon oregano
1 teaspoon thyme
1 teaspoon salt

Sauté 1 onion and 1 stalk of celery in 1 tablespoon oil. When the onion is tender add the rest of the oil and the tempeh, and stir fry until the tempeh is brown, about 10 minutes. Stir in the remaining onion and celery, water, ketchup, green peppers, soy sauce, garlic, oregano, thyme, and salt. Reduce the heat and simmer for another 15 minutes, stirring often to prevent sticking. Serve over cooked pasta.

Serves 4

Per serving: Calories: 283, Protein: 12 gm., Fat: 10 gm., Carbohydrates: 34 gm.

Soups and Stews

Windward Island Pumpkin or Squash Soup

- ½ lb firm tofu, cut in ½-inch cubes
- 2 tablespoons soy sauce
- 2 teaspoons black pepper
- 3 small onions, chopped
- 4 cloves garlic, minced
- 2 stalks celery, chopped
- 2 sprigs fresh parsley, chopped
- 1 sprig thyme
- 1 teaspoon oil
- 2 lbs pumpkin or winter squash
- 5 cups water
- 1 teaspoon oil
- 2 cups soymilk
- 2 cups whole cooked soybeans
- 2 teaspoons salt

Marinate the tofu in soy sauce and pepper. Sauté the onions, garlic, celery, parsley, and thyme in 1 teaspoon oil. Wash, peel, and cut the pumpkin or squash into small pieces. In a large pot, cook the pumpkin in the water until soft. Blend or mash the pumpkin. Sauté the tofu in 1 teaspoon oil. Add the tofu, vegetables, soymilk, soybeans, and salt, and to the pumpkin. Continue cooking, adding more water or soymilk to main-tain the desired consistency. Dumplings and other vegetables can also be added.

Serves 6

Per serving: Calories: 237, Protein: 15 gm., Fat: 8 gm., Carbohydrates: 22 gm.

Calalou Soup

¾ lb firm tofu, cut into ½-inch cubes
2 tablespoons soy sauce
2 teaspoons black pepper
½ lb calalou (page 10) or fresh spinach
2 small onions, chopped
2 cloves garlic, minced
3 stalks celery, chopped
4 sprigs fresh parsley, chopped
1 sprig fresh thyme
1 teaspoon oil
5 cups water
1½ cups coconut milk
2 teaspoons salt

Marinate the tofu in the soy sauce and pepper. Wash the calalou leaves or spinach, cut, blanch in water, and drain. In a large pot, sauté the onions, garlic, celery, parsley, and thyme in the oil. Add the calalou and sauté a few more minutes. Add the water, coconut milk, salt, and cook for 5 minutes. Blend ¾ of the mixture, return to the pot, add the tofu, and simmer for 10 more minutes.

Serves 6

Per serving: Calories: 210, Protein: 6 gm., Fat: 16 gm., Carbohydrates: 7 gm.

Jamaica Stew

¼ cup bell pepper, chopped
½ cup tomato sauce
¼ cup soy sauce
2 cloves garlic, minced
1 tablespoon sugar
1½ teaspoons salt
½ teaspoon fresh gingerroot, grated
1 lb firm tofu, cubed
½ cup unbleached white flour
2 tablespoons oil
½ cup green beans, chopped
½ cup carrots, diced
3 cups water
2 tablespoons whole wheat flour

In a bowl, combine the bell pepper, tomato sauce, soy sauce, garlic, sugar, salt, and ginger. Add the tofu and marinate overnight in a refrigerator. Remove the tofu from the marinade, dip in it the white flour, and fry in the oil until golden brown on all sides. Cook the green beans and carrots in the water until just tender, and add the remaining marinade. Mix the whole wheat flour with ¼ cup of the vegetable water, add to vegetables, and cook for 5 minutes. Stir in the tofu cubes, and serve with rice and whole wheat bread.

Serves 6

Per serving: Calories: 340, Protein: 9 gm., Fat: 9 gm., Carbohydrates: 56 gm.

Caribbean Tempeh Sanoche

This dish is traditionally made with a whole blended coconut.

4 cups calalou (page 10) or spinach, chopped
1 teaspoon salt
1 lb tempeh, cubed
4 tablespoons soy sauce
1 tablespoon nutritional yeast
1 teaspoon coriander
2 tablespoons oil
2 lbs tanias (page 14) or potatoes
2 medium onions, chopped
3 sweet peppers, chopped
6 cloves garlic, diced
3 stalks celery, diced
5 ounces coconut milk
1 teaspoon paprika

Clean, wash, and chop the calalou or spinach into small pieces. Cover with water, add the salt, and boil for 20 minutes. While the calalou is cooking, marinate the tempeh in the soy sauce, nutritional yeast, and coriander. Remove the tempeh from the marinade, and sauté in the oil until golden brown. Mash or blend the cooked calalou. Add the remaining tempeh marinade, tanias or potatoes, onions, sweet peppers, garlic, and celery, and boil for another 10 minutes. When the tanias or potatoes are soft, add the coconut milk, and paprika.

Serves 6 to 8

Per serving: Calories: 360, Protein: 15 gm., Fat: 13 gm., Carbohydrates: 44 gm.

Rastafari Drot

Our Rastafarian friends call this a "drot." Its a flavorful, nutritious, and filling midday meal.

½ lb cooked black-eyed peas
1 lb firm tofu, cubed
1 lb dasheen, tania, (page 11) or potato, chopped
1 medium onion, chopped
1 cup calalou or spinach, diced
1 cup coconut milk
1 sprig fresh parsley, chopped
½ teaspoon dry thyme
1 teaspoon fresh gingerroot, minced
salt and black pepper to taste

Combine all of the ingredients and enough water to make a stew-like consistency. Cook over low heat until the potatoes are cooked. Serve with hot whole wheat or corn bread.

Serves 4

Per serving: Calories: 414, Protein: 15 gm., Fat: 18 gm., Carbohydrates: 44 gm.

Sandwiches and Burgers

Tofu Pollo

- ½ lb firm tofu, frozen
- 1 clove garlic, crushed
- 1 tablespoon soy sauce
- 1 tablespoon nutritional yeast
- 1 teaspoon poultry seasoning
- 1 teaspoon lime juice
- 3 tablespoons unbleached white flour

Freeze the tofu overnight in a plastic bag without water. Thaw the tofu, press out any excess water, and cut into slices. You can thaw the bagged frozen tofu more quickly by placing it in a bowl of hot water, replacing the water as necessary until thawing is complete. Marinate the tofu in the soy sauce, nutritional yeast, poultry seasoning, and lime juice for approximately 30 minutes. Preheat the oven to 350°F. Coat each slice with flour, and bake on a lightly oiled cookie sheet, turning once until golden brown on both sides, approximately 40 minutes. Serve with sautéed onion rings in a sandwich with your favorite fixings.

Makes 6 slices

Per slice: Calories: 50, Protein: 4 gm., Fat: 1 gm., Carbohydrates: 4 gm.

Okara Burgers

- 1 cup okara (page 13) or grated tofu
- ½ cup whole wheat flour
- 1 onion, diced
- 1 stalk celery, diced
- 1 carrot, grated
- 1 clove garlic, crushed
- ½ sprig fresh thyme
- ½ teaspoon salt
- ½ teaspoon curry powder
- ½ teaspoon turmeric
- ½ teaspoon hot pepper sauce
- oil for frying

Mix all of the ingredients, except the oil for frying, and form into patties. Fry in hot oil on both sides until golden brown. Serve on your favorite sandwich bun.

Makes 6 to 8 burgers

Per burger: Calories: 55, Protein: 2 gm., Fat: 0 gm., Carbohydrates: 11 gm.

Seaside Tempeh

- 1 lb tempeh, cut into 1-inch strips
- ¼ cup soy sauce
- ¼ cup coconut milk
- 2 teaspoons lime juice
- 2 cloves garlic, crushed
- 1 teaspoon black pepper
- 1 sprig fresh parsley, chopped
- 2 small onions
- oil for frying

Steam the tempeh for 5 minutes, and drain. Dice 1 of the onions, and mix with the soy sauce, coconut milk, lime juice, garlic, pepper, and parsley. Marinate the tempeh in the mix for 1 hour. Drain and fry the tempeh in hot oil until golden on both sides. Cut the remaining onion in rings, sauté in oil, and serve over the tempeh.

Serves 8

Per serving: Calories: 140, Protein: 10 gm., Fat: 5 gm., Carbohydrates: 12 gm.

Rainforest Campfire Fry

- 1½ cups corn meal
- 1 teaspoon salt
- 1 teaspoon black pepper
- 1 clove garlic, diced
- 1 teaspoon favorite herbs
- 1 lb firm tofu, sliced ½ inch thick
- oil for frying
- 2 tablespoons fresh gingerroot, grated

In a bowl, mix the corn meal, salt, pepper, garlic, and your favorite herbs. Dip the tofu in the mix, and fry in a small amount of hot oil until golden brown on one side. Flip the tofu, sprinkle the grated ginger between the slices, and fry until golden brown. Serve with rice or potatoes.

Serves 3 to 4

Per serving: Calories: 313, Protein: 14 gm., Fat: 6 gm., Carbohydrates: 49 gm.

Nature Island Spread

½ lb tempeh
1 tablespoon oil
2 cloves garlic, minced
1 tablespoon soy sauce
¼ cup fresh parsley, chopped
3 tablespoons fresh lime juice
1½ teaspoons spicy mustard
½ cup bell pepper, chopped

Steam the tempeh for 20 minutes, cool, and cut into small pieces. Combine all of the ingredients, except the bell pepper, and mix in a blender. Remove from the blender and add the chopped green pepper. Cover and chill for several hours before serving. This is a good spread for crackers or breads.

Makes approximately 1½ cups

Per 2 tablespoons: Calories: 50, Protein: 3 gm., Fat: 2 gm., Carbohydrates: 4 gm.

Tokara Sandwich Filling

1 lb tofu or tokara (page 14), grated
2 small tomatoes, chopped
2 medium onions, chopped
1 large sweet pepper, diced
¼ lb cabbage, chopped
1 stalk celery, chopped
1 chive, chopped
2 sprigs fresh parsley, chopped
1 sprig fresh thyme, chopped
2 cloves garlic, minced
1 tablespoon hot pepper sauce
2 tablespoons soy sauce
1 teaspoon salt
2 tablespoons oil

Sauté all of the ingredients in the oil for 15 minutes. Use as a filling for sandwiches, pies, etc.

Makes approximately 3 cups

Per ¼ cup: Calories: 64, Protein: 3 gm., Fat: 4 gm., Carbohydrates: 4 gm.

Drinks

Rainforest Coffee

2 cups soybeans
8 whole cloves
1 tablespoon nutmeg
1 vanilla bean
1 teaspoon chocolate milk mix or cocoa
  powder
honey or other sweetener

Soak the soybeans for 5 hours and drain. Preheat the oven to 300°F. Roast the soybeans on a cookie sheet until almost black, stirring occasionally. Grind the beans very fine in a coffee mill, grain mill, or blender, when hot if possible. Then grind the cloves, nutmeg, and vanilla bean together until they are very fine. Add the chocolate powder. Mix all ingredients thoroughly. Use about 1 large tablespoon of mixture for each cup of hot water. Add sweetener and cream to taste.

Makes approximately 1 cup of mix

Per tablespoon dry mix: Calories: 38, Protein: 3 gm., Fat: 1 gm., Carbohydrates: 2 gm.

Windward Tropic Shakes

4 cups fruit—passion fruit, guava, pine
  apple, papaya, soursop, sugar
  apple, custard apple, or star fruit
  (carambula) (page 14)
4 cups soymilk
¼ cup fresh lime juice
½ cup sugar or honey
1 tablespoon oil
1 tablespoon vanilla
crushed ice

Wash the fruit. Blend all of the ingredients together, add crushed ice, and enjoy.

Serves 4

Per serving: Calories: 280, Protein: 6 gm., Fat: 8 gm., Carbohydrates: 46 gm.

Menta Coffee

2 cups soybeans
1 tablespoon dried spearmint or pepper-
**   mint**
honey or other sweetener

Soak the soybeans for 5 hours, and drain. Preheat the oven to 300°F. Roast the soybeans on a cookie sheet until almost black, stirring occasionally. Grind the dark roasted soybeans and mint together to a fine consistency in a coffee mill, grain mill, or blender. Use about 1 large tablespoon of mixture for each cup of hot water. Add sweetener to taste. This drink can be served hot or iced, as is the custom in the Caribbean.

Makes approximately
one cup of mix

Per tablespoon dry mix: Calories: 37, Protein: 3 gm., Fat: 1 gm., Carbohydrates: 2 gm.

Snacks

Accras

- **1 lb tofu, grated**
- **4 cloves garlic, crushed**
- **2 medium green onions, chopped**
- **½ cup fresh parsley, chopped**
- **2 tablespoons soy sauce**
- **1 tablespoon curry powder**
- **1½ teaspoons baking powder**
- **1 tablespoon dry thyme**
- **1 teaspoon salt**
- **½ cup water**
- **½ cup whole wheat flour**
- **1 cup unbleached white flour**

In a large bowl, combine all of the ingredients, except the water and flour, and mix well. Add the water and gradually add the flour, mixing thoroughly to ensure that there are no lumps. Shape into small bars using a fork and your finger (they should be about ½ inch thick, 1½ inches wide, and 3 inches long). Bake in the oven at 350°F on a well greased cookie sheet, or fry in very hot oil until golden brown and crispy.

Makes approximately 14 accras

Per accra: Calories: 70, Protein: 4 gm., Fat: 1 gm., Carbohydrates: 10 gm.

Soya Bakes

- **3¼ cups whole wheat flour**
- **¾ cup soy flour**
- **2 tablespoons baking powder**
- **1 teaspoon salt**
- **¼ cup oil**
- **1⅓ cups water**

Sift together the flours, baking powder, and salt. Add the oil and water, and mix thoroughly. Knead the dough until smooth. Cut pieces from the dough, roll into balls, and flatten out. Deep fry until golden brown. These are a traditional Caribbean snack eaten with Accras (page 50), or fruit juice.

Makes 32

Per serving: Calories: 67, Protein: 2 gm., Fat: 2 gm., Carbohydrates: 10 gm.

Hot Hot Hot Creole Crunch

1 lb soybeans
oil for frying
1 teaspoon curry powder
1 teaspoon dry hot peppers, finely
    ground
1 teaspoon garlic powder
1 teaspoon ground ginger
salt to taste

Soak the soybeans for 5 hours. Drain, rinse, and thoroughly dry. Heat the oil in a skillet until very hot. Fry the soybeans until golden brown, about 10 to 15 minutes. Remove and drain on paper towels. Mix the seasonings, sprinkle on the soybeans to taste, and mix well.

Makes 3 cups

Per 2 tablespoons: Calories: 33, Protein: 3 gm., Fat: 1 gm., Carbohydrates: 2 gm.

Banana Fritters

1 cup cooked soybeans (page 16)
¾ cup water (from cooking beans)
½ ripe banana, mashed
1 cup unbleached white flour
¼ onion, chopped
½ clove garlic, crushed
½ teaspoon salt
1 teaspoon curry powder
½ teaspoon turmeric
2 teaspoons baking powder
½ teaspoon pepper
oil for cooking

Mash about ⅔ of the soybeans. Add the rest of the soybeans, all of the other ingredients, and mix well. The batter should be quite thick. Drop by spoonfuls into hot oil, and fry until golden brown.

Makes 12 fritters

Per fritter: Calories: 64, Protein: 3 gm., Fat: 1 gm., Carbohydrates: 10 gm.

Baby's Tropical Delight

¾ cup soymilk
⅛ lb tofu
2 large tablespoons fresh papaya
**   or ½ ripe banana**
½ teaspoon sugar or honey

Combine all of the ingredients, and blend at high speed until creamy. Serve immediately.

Makes 1 cup

Per ½ cup: Calories: 82, Protein: 4 gm., Fat: 2 gm., Carbohydrates: 8 gm.

Desserts

Coconut Corn Pudding

1 cup cornmeal
½ cup soy flour
½ cup unbleached white flour
¼ teaspoon salt
¼ cup soymilk
1 cup sugar
1 teaspoon vanilla
½ teaspoon ground cinnamon
½ teaspoon ground nutmeg
3 cups coconut milk

Sift together the cornmeal, soy flour, white flour, and salt. Add soymilk, a little at a time, to moisten the dry mixture. The mixture should be stiff. Preheat the oven to 350°F. Add the sugar, vanilla, cinnamon, and nutmeg to the coconut milk, and bring to a boil. Pour the heated coconut milk over the flour mixture, stirring vigorously with a wire whisk to prevent lumps. Pour the mixture into a casserole dish, and bake for about 45 minutes. Cool before serving.

Serves 8

Per serving: Calories: 421, Protein: 6 gm., Fat: 22 gm., Carbohydrates: 49 gm.

Mango Pudding

A nice light dessert or treat.

2 cups mangoes, peeled and chopped
½ lb tofu, cubed
½ cup honey or sugar
1 tablespoon vanilla
2 teaspoons oil
dash of salt

Combine all of the ingredients in a blender, and blend until smooth and creamy. Pour into small bowls and chill for several hours before serving.

Serves 6

Per serving: Calories: 165, Protein: 3 gm., Fat: 3 gm., Carbohydrates: 31 gm.

Sweet Potato and Coconut Pudding

½ lb sweet potatoes, cubed (1 cup mashed)
1 cup soymilk
1 cup coconut milk
¾ cup sugar
1 tablespoon flour
1 tablespoon cornstarch
1 tablespoon soy flour
1 teaspoon fresh gingerroot, grated
1 teaspoon cinnamon

Boil, drain, and mash the sweet potatoes. Preheat the oven to 350°F. Mix in the remaining ingredients, stirring until well blended, and pour into an oiled, medium baking dish. Bake for 45 minutes to 1 hour.

Serves 6

Per serving: Calories: 158, Protein: 2 gm., Fat: 2 gm., Carbohydrates: 35 gm.

Banana Tofu Cream Pie

Tofu adds more body and nutrients than found in traditional banana pie.

1 cup mashed bananas
2½ teaspoons vanilla
1 tablespoon lime juice
1 teaspoon oil
¾ cup sugar
½ teaspoon salt
3 cups tofu
prebaked pie crust

Blend the bananas, vanilla, lime juice, oil, sugar, and salt. Gradually add the tofu and blend until the mixture is creamy and smooth. Pour the mixture into a prebaked, medium pie crust, and chill for several hours.

Serves 8

Per serving: Calories: 274, Protein: 8 gm., Fat: 12 gm., Carbohydrates: 33 gm.

Breadnut Pudding

4 cups soymilk
⅔ cup sugar
1 tablespoon vanilla
1 teaspoon cinnamon
1 teaspoon nutmeg
1 teaspoon allspice
½ teaspoon salt
1 cup breadnuts (page 10) or new
    potatoes, cooked and grated
4 cups whole wheat bread, torn into
    small pieces

Preheat the oven to 350°F. Mix all of the ingredients together, adding the pieces of bread last. Pour into an oiled, medium baking dish, and bake for 20 minutes.

Serves 8

Per serving: Calories: 153, Protein: 5 gm., Fat: 3 gm., Carbohydrates: 27 gm.

Coconutty Cookies

½ cup margarine
1 ½ cups sugar
2 cups firm tofu, grated
1 cup coconut flakes
½ cup soymilk
2 teaspoons vanilla
2 cups unbleached white flour
4 teaspoons baking powder
1 teaspoon allspice
1 teaspoon nutmeg
1 teaspoon cinnamon
½ teaspoon salt

Preheat the oven to 350°F. Cream the margarine with the sugar and add the tofu, coconut, soymilk, and vanilla. In a separate bowl, mix together the flour, baking powder, allspice, nutmeg, cinnamon, and salt. Add the flour mixture to the wet mixture, blending thoroughly. Drop by spoonfuls onto a lightly oiled baking sheet, and press down with a fork. (Occasionally dipping the fork in cold water will help to keep it from sticking.) Bake for 15 to 20 minutes or until golden brown on top.

Makes 24 cookies

Per cookie: Calories: 192, Protein: 3 gm., Fat: 10 gm., Carbohydrates: 21 gm.

Pineapple Muffins

5½ cups unbleached white flour
2½ cups sugar
4½ tablespoons baking powder
1 tablespoon ground cinnamon
1 tablespoon ground allspice
1 tablespoon ground nutmeg
¼ teaspoon salt
3 cups tofu, grated
1½ cups soymilk
1½ cups pineapple, minced
2 tablespoons vanilla
1 tablespoon oil

Preheat the oven to 350°F. In a large bowl, sift together the flour, sugar, baking powder, cinnamon, allspice, nutmeg, and salt. Mix the tofu, soymilk, pineapple, vanilla, and oil together, add to the dry ingredients, and mix just until the dry ingredients are moist. Pour into lightly oiled muffin tins, and bake for 30 minutes or until golden brown.

Makes 36 muffins

Per muffin: Calories: 137, Protein: 4 gm., Fat: 1 gm., Carbohydrates: 27 gm.

Dominican Ground Nut Fudge Delight

3 cups sugar
1 cup soymilk
1½ tablespoons oil
2 cups firm tofu, grated
½ cup roasted peanuts, halved or
    chopped
2 teaspoons vanilla

Boil the sugar, soymilk, and oil steadily until the mixture forms a soft ball when dropped in cold water. During cooking, brush the inside of the cooking pot with cold water to prevent graining, and stir very carefully to prevent burning. Add the tofu, stir, and cook for 5 more minutes. Remove from the heat and add the peanuts and vanilla. Beat until the fudge is thick and creamy, and pour into a well greased, medium baking pan. When set, cut into squares and cool.

Serves 9

Per serving: Calories: 358, Protein: 6 gm., Fat: 8 gm., Carbohydrates: 63 gm.

Guava Cake

This cake tastes even better the next day.

½ cup oil
½ cup sugar
1½ cups guava (page 12), peeled and chopped
1 cup water
½ cup firm tofu, grated
2 cups unbleached white flour
¼ cup soy flour
2 teaspoons baking powder
1 teaspoon cinnamon or nutmeg
1 teaspoon salt
1 cup soymilk

Mix the oil and sugar well. Put the guavas in a small saucepan with the water, bring to a boil, and stir over low heat until they cook into a thick liquid. Add the guava to the oil and sugar, and mix well. Preheat the oven to 350°F. Add the tofu, white flour, soy flour, baking powder, cinnamon or nutmeg, salt, and soymilk, and beat until smooth. Pour into an oiled and floured 8-inch cake pan, and bake for 45–50 minutes.

Serves 8

Per serving: Calories: 318, Protein: 6 gm., Fat: 15 gm., Carbohydrates: 38 gm.

Antilles Spiced Banana Cake

1½ cups whole wheat flour
½ cup soy flour
1 tablespoon baking powder
1 teaspoon salt
1 teaspoon cinnamon
1 teaspoon nutmeg
¼ cup margarine
¾ cup brown sugar
1 cup ripe bananas, mashed
6 tablespoons soymilk
1 teaspoon vanilla
1 teaspoon lime juice
1 teaspoon lime rind, grated

Sift together the flours, baking powder, salt, cinnamon, and nutmeg. In another bowl, mix the margarine, sugar, and bananas. Preheat the oven to 350°F. Mix together the soymilk, vanilla, lime juice, and lime rind. Add the flour alternating with the soymilk to the banana mixture. Stir until well blended only. Pour the batter into an oiled, medium baking pan, and bake for approximately 30 minutes.

Serves 8

Per serving: Calories: 229, Protein: 6 gm., Fat: 7 gm., Carbohydrates: 34 gm.

Central America

The people, geography, and politics of the Central American region are extraordinarily diverse. Each country, from tiny El Salvador to multi-cultural Belize, has a unique history which has helped shaped its physical, social, cultural, and political landscape.

Many of the traditional Central American recipes included in this section have been staples for families of all economic classes for generations. Some of these recipes, adapted to include soy foods, are made in their country of origin using the milky fiber residue *okara* (page 11) that is leftover from the process of making tofu or soymilk. Known as *payana* in Nicaragua or *parche* in Belize, okara contains approximately 5 percent protein as well as fiber, vitamins, and minerals. Because most people in North America do not make their own soymilk or tofu at home, okara can be hard to find. We have replaced the okara in some recipes with grated tofu or tempeh.

Since the late 1970s, Plenty has worked with people from many Central American cultures in their efforts to evolve primary health care systems, sustainable agriculture, crafts and weaving enterprises, village eco-tourism, and food processing businesses.

Belize

Belize is one of the most unspoiled areas of land in the world. Its rain forests, savannas, Mayan ruins, and 180 miles of living barrier reef have remained largely unexplored by foreign tourists, but this is changing. History has endowed Belize with a mix of cultures including Mayan, Garifuna (African-Amerindian), Creole, Hispanic, and European, all of which have contributed to the diverse cuisine one can find when visiting there.

Soy Promotion in Belize

In the early months of 1991, Plenty was asked by representatives of the Caribbean Organization of Indigenous People (COIP) to assist some of Belize's Garifuna and Mayan communities in small economic development projects. At the same time, Plenty was receiving requests from farming cooperatives and women's groups who wanted to learn more about growing, processing, and marketing soybeans. From the beginning of September until December of that year, I had the wonderful opportunity of traveling and working in villages throughout most of this beautiful country.

During this time, a conference sponsored by the Caribbean Agriculture Research and Development Institute (CARDI) and the government of Belize took place which focused on ways in which Belize could sustain its own food needs. It was designed to be an exchange of ideas between farming families, researchers, business leaders, and government personnel. I was asked by the director of CARDI to prepare a variety of traditional foods utilizing soy-

beans for conference participants. We contacted several of the women's and farmer's groups Plenty had been working with to see if they could help, and they readily agreed. On the last day of the conference, Hispanic, Garifuna, Creole, and Mayan women worked together to prepare a variety of soy-based foods—*tamalitos*, *garnachas*, vegetarian pot pies, and cakes. These delicious foods, familiar yet different, helped convince even the most skeptical observers that soybeans had the potential to become an important food source for the people of Belize.

Chuck Haren

Guatemalan Farmers Face Serious Challenges

Mayan subsistence farmers in rural Guatemala are attempting to support a growing population on a limited amount of land. With each generation, family plots of land, most of which already do not produce a year's supply of food, are further subdivided. Every year rural farmers must clear more marginal land to raise their traditional crops of *maize* (corn) and beans. This increases deforestation and erosion. Loss of topsoil results in lower crop yields, forcing farmers to clear even more land to plant, which continues this destructive cycle.

Mayans have not always been faced with this dilemma. In pre-colonial times there was sufficient fertile land to farm. Now much of Guatemala's fertile lands produce nonfood and luxury crops for export, which contribute nothing toward feeding the country's mostly rural population.

In addition, rural Guatemala is dangerously dependent on two primary food crops, corn and beans. A widespread failure of either of these crops would cause immeasurable suffering. By establishing a wider agricultural base, including soybeans and amaranth (a traditional Mayan high protein grain), families in the Guatemalan highlands can have both a more complete diet and a margin of safety against crop failures.

A Volunteer's Story

I smell the coffee boiling as I walk up the path to Elena's house. She comes out smiling and we hold hands, and eyes too, as we talk. I ask her how her day's been going, and she says it's been happy (she always does). Inside we kneel on straw and pat soft yellow corn tortillas. They cook quickly on the hot clay griddle resting on rocks that surround the crackling fire. I love to hear Elena laugh as we exchange stories and news. She sits so gracefully on the dirt floor, nursing her little one as she pats tortillas.

One time we were talking about God and going to church. Elena said, "We believe that God is in all places. There is one spirit in all the people. We look at the trees and God is there. We look at the rocks and God is there. God is in all the people."

As we wait for the food to cook I comb and braid her little girls' hair. The kids put on my sandals and shuffle around pretending they're me. They sit in my lap, hang all over me, teasing and laughing, asking me words in English, seeing what I have in my pockets, making me feel like one of the family.

We eat, sitting in a half-circle around the fire, Elena serving everyone steaming hot black beans from an earthenware pot. We scoop up the beans with hot tortillas from a basket in the middle. The food is so good and simple and nicely served, it doesn't need to be anything fancy. Elena keeps saying, *"Kishway!"* (Eat, everybody!) And we answer, *"Matiosh, Ka wa rit."* (Thanks, you eat too.) We finish up with big tin cups of coffee, hot and sweet and black. As each person finishes, even the smallest child, they thank the mother, and then each person in the room, going around the circle one by one. Each person smiles and answers in turn. We gather up the dishes and take them out to the faucet to wash.

We sit in the sun outside for awhile, looking at the big blue lake, watching little white clouds collect around the volcanoes. We call out greetings and jokes to the people passing by on the path down at the bottom of the yard — ladies coming home from the market with baskets of food balanced on their heads, men with big loads of firewood strapped on their backs. The radio is on, playing loud marimba music, while the kids run around playing ball. When I come here I feel so much like part of the family that I can hardly stand to leave. Only after lots of good-byes and hand squeezing am I finally off down the soft dirt path towards my house. Elena calls out the traditional good-bye of her people, *"Tatsu abey! N'katasak ta!"* (Look at the road! Don't fall down!)

Jenny Bryant

Nicaragua

Nicaragua is a country with a large international community. In Managua, the capital, there is a myriad of small restaurants frequented by visitors from Germany, Holland, France, Italy, Canada, The United States, England, Eastern Europe, China, Cuba, Spain, Mexico, and all of South and Central America. Although the majority of Nicaragua's population speaks Spanish, you will find large, indigenous Misquito, Rama, and Afro-Caribbean cultures on the Atlantic Coast, a Swiss chalet hotel in Matagalpa, and an October Fest celebrated in Boaco where Germans settled more than 100 years ago.

Casta Calderon's First Experience with Soy Foods

After growing up in the small village of San Juan de Limay, I left to work and study at the Universidad Nacional in Managua. Throughout the 1980s, we were having a terrible war in Nicaragua, and it was very difficult for people to get enough food to eat. One weekend I had the opportunity to visit my mother after not having seen her for more than a year. On arriving home, the family was eating a traditional meal of *cuajada* (soft white cheese), beans and tortillas, and mother offered me some. I immediately accepted because I loved the *cuajada*, and it was very expensive and difficult to get in those times. The food was delicious.

When the meal was finished, my mother came very close to me, and with a little naughtiness in her face, asked if I had enjoyed it. I said, "Yes. What is it with you?" She was laughing and then, speaking with the aura of a scientist, she said, "Well, we don't need to buy a farm or have a cow to make *cuajada* now. I have a special formula," and pulled out a handful of soybeans! She then showed me a refrigerator full of different foods she had made from soybeans. She was happy because my father ate the soy foods without asking, "What is that?" He had always been very picky about the foods he ate.

Mother had learned to make soymilk, soy cheese, and *salpicon* (a kind of hash) from people working with a church solidarity group. The people had donated and distributed soybeans throughout the region during the contra war. This was my first exposure to soy foods, but it was not to be my last.

Five years later I met a group of women in Managua who had organized and were conducting education and nutrition programs with children, pregnant women, and nursing mothers. They had a job opening, and I ended up working with the organization they had founded, SOYNICA. While at SOYNICA I learned much more about the value of soybeans. In 1992, SOYNICA asked for Plenty's help in teaching people more about the uses of soybeans and in starting a soy foods processing and marketing business. Plenty sent a technician who cooked soy foods with the same ease that I make traditional Nicaraguan foods. Since my contact with Plenty, I have learned to make many great tasting foods with soybeans. Oh yes, there is one more thing I should tell you. The person they sent is now my husband!

Casta Calderon

Main Dishes

Tamalitos Buenísimos

One of the staple foods in Central America, tamales are prepared with many different combinations of ingredients.

12 ears of fresh, green field corn
4 tablespoons margarine
1 lb firm tofu or tokara, crumbled
2 teaspoons salt
15 green corn leaves

Husk the corn and keep 15 large green leaves. Scrape the corn from the cob, and run it through a grain mill, or chop it in a blender at low speed, just enough to make a fine consistency. Melt the margarine in a small saucepan. In a large bowl, thoroughly mix the corn, tofu or tokara, margarine, and salt. Rinse the corn husks. Add 1 or 2 heaping tablespoons of the corn and soy mixture to each corn husk. Fold the sides and roll up the ends of the corn leaves to hold in the mixture. Stack the tamalitos on a perforated rack or colander inside a large pot with boiling water. Make sure the tamalitos are above the boiling water and that they are stacked to allow the steam to circulate around them. Steam for 30 to 40 minutes. If the tamalitos are wrapped very well, they can also be boiled in water for 30 to 40 minutes. When finished, each tamalito should have a solid, dough-like consistency. Serve with enchiladas, tostadas, taco salads, or just salsa.

Makes 15 tamalitos

Per tamalito: Calories: 118, Protein: 5 gm., Fat: 4 gm., Carbohydrates: 11 gm.

Tacos Ricos

A Belizean variation of a food that provides all the flavor, vitamins, protein, and calories that a good meal should.

1 lb firm tofu or tempeh, crumbled
1 tablespoon oil
1 teaspoon chili powder
1 teaspoon poultry seasoning
1 teaspoon black pepper
1 teaspoon salt
8 corn or small wheat flour tortillas
6 cups cabbage, grated
1 large onion, chopped
2 medium tomatoes, chopped
hot sauce or salsa to taste

Sauté the tofu or tempeh in hot oil with the chili powder, poultry seasoning, black pepper, and salt. Warm the tortillas, and fill with the tofu or tempeh mix. Top with the cabbage, onion, tomatoes, and hot sauce or salsa to taste. Serve with rice and salad for a great lunch or dinner.

Serves 8

Per serving: Calories: 153, Protein: 7 gm., Fat: 5 gm., Carbohydrates: 19 gm.

Gallo Pinto

This daily staple of Nicaragua has a balance of flavors that many people love. It's one of the most delicious ways to eat beans and rice.

3 tablespoons oil
1 small onion, chopped
1 cup cooked red beans
1 cup firm tofu, grated
1 cup cooked rice
1 clove garlic, minced
1 small chili pepper, diced
1 teaspoon salt
Monterey Jack or ranchero cheese
    (page 13), grated

Heat the oil in a large frying pan. Add the onion, cook for 2 minutes, then add the red beans, and cook for 10 minutes. Mix the tofu and rice with the beans, and continue to cook on low heat. Add the garlic, chili pepper, and salt, and cook over low heat for 10 minutes. Top with the cheese and serve with soft, hot corn tortillas and salad or cooked vegetables.

Serves 6 to 8

Per serving: Calories: 183, Protein: 7 gm., Fat: 10 gm., Carbohydrates: 16 gm.

Nacatamales

One of these makes a great nutritious lunch time meal for children or adults.

- ¼ lb rice
- ½ lb tempeh, cut in 8 strips
- 1 tablespoon oil
- 4 medium potatoes, chopped
- 4 medium tomatoes, chopped
- 2 medium onions, chopped
- 2 medium bell peppers, chopped
- 4 cloves garlic, minced
- ½ lb firm tofu or tempeh, grated
- 1½ cups masa harina (page 12)
- 1 cup soymilk
- 2 teaspoons salt
- 2 tablespoons oil
- juice of ½ lemon
- 16 banana or corn or grape leaves
- 40 mint leaves

Soak the rice in water for 1 hour. Fry the tempeh in 1 tablespoon oil until golden, and set aside. Boil 2 potatoes until soft. In a blender, mix half of the tomatoes, onions, bell peppers, and all of the garlic. In a large saucepan, mix the blended ingredients with the grated tofu or tempeh, masa harina, the rest of the potatoes, soymilk, salt, and oil. Simmer together for 20 minutes, and add the lemon juice. Wash and steam 16 corn, banana, or grape leaves. Put 2 leaves together, place ½ cup of the seasoned corn dough in the middle, then make a depression and fill with a spoonful of rice, a strip of fried tempeh, a little of each of the remaining vegetables, and 5 mint leaves. Wrap the filling in the leaves, and tie them closed with string or plant fiber. Stack the nacatamales on a perforated rack or colander inside a large pot with boiling water. Make sure the nacatamales are above the boiling water and that they are stacked to allow the steam to circulate around them. Steam for 1 hour. They are done when they are firm. If they are wrapped very well, they can be boiled in water for 1 hour.

Makes 8 nacatamales

Per nacatamale: Calories: 345, Protein: 12 gm., Fat: 9 gm., Carbohydrates: 52 gm.

Salpicón

(vegetarian hash)

An excellent meal you can prepare in 15 minutes.

3 cups firm tofu or tempeh, grated or crumbled
1 small onion, finely chopped
1 medium tomato, finely chopped
1 small bell pepper, finely chopped
½ teaspoon salt
¼ teaspoon black pepper
juice of ½ lime

Squeeze excess water from the tofu. Toast the tofu in a dry, medium-sized, nonstick frying pan, stirring often until it is very light brown. If you don't use a nonstick, pan you may need to add a little water to the tofu when browning. Add all of the vegetables, and mix thoroughly. Stir in the salt, black pepper, and lime juice. Cook on low heat for another 5 minutes. Serve hot or cold as a side dish with rice or potatoes and green or yellow vegetables.

Serves 4

Per serving: Calories: 159, Protein: 13 gm., Fat: 8 gm., Carbohydrates: 7 gm.

Chorizo

(vegetarian sausage)

Central Americans enjoy this popular food over rice or bread with a vegetable and a tall glass of fruit juice.

2 cups tofu or tempeh, grated or crumbled
1 small onion, chopped
1 bell pepper, chopped
1 or 2 cloves of garlic, diced
1 tablespoon oil
juice of ½ small lime
1 teaspoon cumin

Place the tofu or tempeh in a clean cloth, and squeeze out the excess liquid. Blend or hand mill together the onion, bell pepper, and garlic. Sauté the blended ingredients in the oil, and stir in the tofu or tempeh. Add the lime juice and cumin, and cook for another 10 minutes. Chorizo can be used to fill sandwiches, tacos, burritos, tostadas, or served with rice and a salad.

Serves 4

Per serving: Calories: 136, Protein: 9 gm., Fat: 8 gm., Carbohydrates: 5 gm.

Guiso de Pipian o Ayote

(squash or pumpkin stew)

2 cups tempeh or firm tofu, grated
2 tablespoons oil
1 small onion, diced
1 clove garlic, diced
2 small tender yellow squash or
 zucchini, chopped
1 small sprig fresh parsley, chopped
1 teaspoon salt
½ teaspoon black pepper
¾ cup soymilk

Sauté the tempeh in hot oil until golden. Add the onion and garlic, and sauté for 10 more minutes. Mix in the squash or zucchini, parsley, salt, and black pepper, and cook until the squash is soft. Add the soymilk and simmer for 5 more minutes or until most of the liquid is absorbed. Serve with baked potatoes, rice, or your favorite toasted bread.

Serves 4

Per serving: Calories: 265, Protein: 15 gm., Fat: 13 gm., Carbohydrates: 20 gm.

Picadillo de Verduras

(vegetable and tempeh hash)

1 cup firm tofu or tempeh, grated
2 tablespoons oil
½ small onion, chopped
2 cloves garlic, minced
1 green bell pepper, chopped
1 cup water
1 carrot, grated
1 cup cabbage, grated
1 medium tomato, chopped
1 small, yellow squash, chopped
1 small chayote (page 11) or potato,
 chopped
1 teaspoon salt
1 teaspoon black pepper
1 sprig fresh parsley, minced
1 stem fresh cilantro, minced

In a large skillet, sauté the tofu or tempeh in the oil until light brown. Add the onion, garlic, and bell pepper, and sauté for 3 more minutes. Mix in the water and all of the remaining vegetables, and cook on low heat for 5 minutes. Add the salt, black pepper, parsley, and cilantro, and cook until all of the vegetables are soft.

Serves 6

Per serving: Calories: 116, Protein: 4 gm., Fat: 6 gm., Carbohydrates: 11 gm.

Appetizers and Snacks

Garnachas

Light and flavorful tostadas from Belize.

⅔ cup red beans
⅔ cup soybeans
1 clove garlic, chopped
1 teaspoon salt
15 soft corn tortillas
oil for frying
¼ lb white ranchero cheese (page 13)
    or Parmesan cheese, grated
2 medium tomatoes, chopped

Pressure cook the red beans and soybeans together for 60 minutes with the garlic and salt. Drain the cooked beans and mash them into a paste. Lightly fry the tortillas in the oil on both sides until crisp. On each tortilla spread a layer of mashed beans, and top with cheese and tomatoes.

Serves 15

Per serving: Calories: 120, Protein: 6 gm., Fat: 4 gm., Carbohydrates: 15 gm.

Tortas de Papa, Yucca o Camote

(potato cakes)

1 lb white potatoes, yucca (page 15), or
    sweet potatoes, peeled
½ cup tofu or tempeh, grated
½ cup unbleached white flour
1 tablespoon nutritional yeast flakes
    (page 12) (optional)
1 teaspoon salt
1 tablespoon vegetable oil

Boil the white potatoes, yucca, or sweet potatoes whole, and when soft, break apart into pieces. Mix with the tofu or tempeh, ¼ cup of flour, nutritional yeast, and salt. Make small, round patty cakes or *tortas* 2 inches across by ½ inch thick. Bread the patties with the remaining flour, and cook on a lightly oiled, hot skillet until golden brown on both sides. Serve with salad or cooked vegetables.

Serves 4

Per serving: Calories: 201, Protein: 5 gm., Fat: 5 gm., Carbohydrates: 34 gm.

Buñuelos de Yucca

1 lb yucca (page 15) or potatoes, peeled
1 cup tofu, grated or crumbled
1 cup ranchero cheese (page 13) or
    Monterey Jack cheese, grated
⅔ cup unbleached white flour
oil for frying
honey for dipping

With a grinder or grain mill, grind the yucca or potatoes to a coarse texture. If you do not have a mill or grinder, cook until soft, and mash. Mix in a bowl with the tofu and cheese. If you do not use yucca, mix in the flour. Mix the dough well, and form into small, round, ½-inch thick tortas. Fry in hot oil on both sides until slightly crispy. Drain the excess oil, dip the tortas in honey, and serve.

Serves 10

Per serving: Calories: 127, Protein: 6 gm., Fat: 4 gm., Carbohydrates: 15 gm.

Salads and Dressings

Granada Vigoron

1 lb yucca (page 15)
  or white potatoes, peeled
1 lb firm tofu
2 teaspoons oil
1 lb cabbage, shredded
2 medium tomatoes, chopped
1 medium carrot, grated
1 small cucumber, chopped
2 limes, sliced
salt to taste
2 small pickled hot peppers, diced

Cook the yucca or potatoes until soft, and cut into bite-sized pieces. Slice the tofu in 2-inch squares, ¼ inch thick. In a large skillet, fry the tofu in the oil until very crispy, almost brittle. Place the yucca or potatoes on salad plates, and arrange a few pieces of tofu on top and to the side. Mix all of the vegetables together, and place them on top of the tofu and potatoes. Add a little lime juice, salt, and hot pepper to the top of each dish. Have a tall glass of iced fruit drink to go with this delicious, light lunchtime meal.

Serves 6 to 8

Per serving: Calories: 151, Protein: 6 gm., Fat: 4 gm., Carbohydrates: 22 gm.

Guacamole Nicaragüense

2 avocados
½ cup ranchero cheese (page 13),
  grated
½ cup firm tofu, grated
½ cup soymilk
1 small onion, chopped
1 clove garlic, minced
1 stem fresh cilantro, chopped
3 tablespoons lemon or lime juice
1 teaspoon salt

In a blender, blend all of the ingredients until smooth. Serve with corn chips, crackers, in burritos, or on tacos.

Makes about 3 cups

Per 2 tablespoons: Calories: 44, Protein: 1 gm., Fat: 3 gm., Carbohydrates: 3 gm.

Mayonesa de Ranchero y Queso de Soya

(soy mayonnaise)

- **1 cup tofu, crumbled**
- **1 tablespoon toasted sesame seeds**
- **¼ cup ranchero cheese (page13), chopped**
- **1 sprig fresh cilantro**
- **4 tablespoons lime juice**
- **1 sprig fresh parsley**
- **1 teaspoon vegetable oil**
- **2 cloves garlic, minced**
- **½ teaspoon salt**
- **1 teaspoon black pepper**

Combine all of the ingredients in a blender, and blend until creamy. Serve as a dip with your favorite snack foods or with your favorite Central American meals.

Makes 1½ cups

Per 2 tablespoons: Calories: 34, Protein: 2 gm., Fat: 3 gm., Carbohydrates: 1 gm.

Soups and Stews

Sopa de Albóndigas

2 cups masa harina (page 12)
1 cup water
1 medium onion, chopped
1 tomato, chopped
1 bell pepper, chopped
1 clove garlic, diced
1 teaspoon oil
2 cups tempeh, grated
1 teaspoon margarine
3 cups water
1 teaspoon dried mint
1 teaspoon oregano
1 teaspoon thyme
½ teaspoon paprika

Make 2 cups of corn masa by adding water a little at a time to the masa harina and kneading until smooth. Sauté the onion, tomato, bell pepper, and garlic together in the oil making a thick stew. Lightly toast the tempeh for 5 minutes in a small frying pan, stirring often. Mix half of the vegetable stew with the corn masa, tempeh, and the margarine to form a dough. To the remaining vegetable stew, add 3 cups water, the mint, oregano, thyme, and paprika, and simmer. Roll the dough into 2-inch balls and add to the soup. Simmer for 20 minutes. Serve with salad and crackers.

Serves 6

Per serving: Calories: 215, Protein: 11 gm., Fat: 5 gm., Carbohydrates: 31 gm.

Sopa de Queso

(cheese soup)

- 1 cup masa harina (page 12)
- ½ cup water
- 1 cup tofu, grated
- 1 cup Monterey Jack cheese, grated
- 1 teaspoon baking powder
- 1 teaspoon salt
- 1 medium onion, chopped
- 3 cloves garlic, minced
- 1 medium bell pepper, chopped
- 2 tablespoons oil
- 2 medium tomatoes, chopped
- 4 cups water
- 1½ teaspoons salt

To make "tortas": Mix the masa harina with ½ cup of water to form a dough. Add the tofu, cheese, baking powder, and 1 teaspoon salt. This makes a soft dough. Blend or mill together half of the onion, garlic, and bell pepper. Mix the blended vegetables thoroughly into the dough. Set aside ½ cup of the dough. Make the remaining dough into small, round (3 inch diameter by ¾ inch thick) patty cakes or "tortas." In a medium frying pan, fry the tortas in the oil until both sides are golden, and set aside. In the same frying pan, sauté the rest of the vegetables, adding a little water if needed to prevent sticking. In a medium saucepan, combine the sautéed vegetables, 4 cups water, and the ½ cup of dough mixture that was set aside, stirring well. Simmer the stew for about 5 minutes, then add the fried tortas, and simmer for 5 more minutes. Serve with a salad, crackers, or your favorite breads.

Serves 5

Per serving: Calories: 296, Protein: 12 gm., Fat: 14 gm., Carbohydrates: 28 gm.

Guiso de Papa

- 2 medium potatoes, peeled
- 1½ cups water
- ¼ cup soy flour
- ¾ cup soymilk
- 1 medium onion, chopped
- 1 clove garlic, minced
- 1 small yellow squash or zucchini, chopped
- 1 teaspoon oil
- 1 sprig fresh parsley, chopped
- 1 teaspoon salt

Cut the potatoes into fourths. In a medium pot, boil the potatoes in the water until soft, and drain. Add the soy flour and soymilk to the potatoes, and stir well. In a medium skillet, sauté the onion, garlic, and squash in the oil. Add the potato mixture, parsley, and salt to the vegetables, and simmer for 5 to 10 minutes. Serve with crackers and a salad.

Serves 4

Per serving: Calories: 134, Protein: 5 gm., Fat: 3 gm., Carbohydrates: 21 gm.

Drinks

Raspado Tamarindo y Miel

(tamarind and honey on ice)

½ cup tamarind concentrate (page 14)
½ cup soymilk
2 tablespoons honey
2 cups ice

In a blender, combine the tamarind, soymilk, and honey. Blend and pour over ice in a tall glass. Stir and eat with a spoon.

Serves 1 to 2

Per serving: Calories: 120, Protein: 2 gm., Fat: 1 gm., Carbohydrates: 25 gm.

Refresco Cacao y Clavo de Olor

(clove and cocoa drink)

3 cups soymilk
1 tablespoon powdered cocoa
½ teaspoon ground cloves
1 teaspoon vanilla
2 tablespoons honey
1 cup ice, crushed

In a blender, combine the soymilk, cocoa, cloves, vanilla, and honey. Blend and serve over crushed ice.

Makes 4 cups

Per cup: Calories: 97, Protein: 5 gm., Fat: 4 gm., Carbohydrates: 12 gm.

Refresco Arroz y Soy Canela

(vanilla, rice, and soy drink)

- **3 cups soymilk**
- **¼ cup rice flour**
- **1 teaspoon vanilla extract**
- **2 tablespoons honey**
- **1 cup ice, crushed**

In a blender, combine the soymilk, rice flour, vanilla, and honey. Blend and serve over crushed ice.

Makes 4 to 5 cups

Per serving: Calories: 129, Protein: 5 gm., Fat: 4 gm., Carbohydrates: 20 gm.

Rosquillas

This is a delicious, light, and flavorful pastry. Serve with coffee, tea, or milk any time.

- **¾ cup whole wheat flour**
- **½ cup finely ground corn meal**
- **¼ cup soy flour**
- **1 tablespoon baking powder**
- **½ teaspoon salt**
- **2 tablespoons oil**
- **⅔ cup water**
- **1 cup ranchero cheese (page 13), grated**
- **2 teaspoons cream**

Preheat the oven to 350°F. In a medium bowl, mix all of the flours, baking powder, and salt. Stir in the oil thoroughly. Add the water, cheese, and cream, and knead into a soft dough. Form into 2-inch balls, and roll out into a ½-inch thick pencil shape. Make a circle with the dough, and connect the ends. Place on an oiled baking pan, and bake for about 20 minutes or until crunchy. You can also form the dough balls into small cups, and fill them with a little fruit or jam half way through the baking.

Makes 10 to 12 rosquillas

Per rosquillas: Calories: 126, Protein: 5 gm., Fat: 6 gm., Carbohydrates: 12 gm.

Desserts

Pan Dulce

(sweet bread)

This high protein recipe, a variation on traditional sweet bread, was developed at a preschool and feeding center for low income children in urban El Salvador. Pan dulce is good served at breakfast with coffee or other hot drinks or for a midday snack.

- 1 cup unbleached white flour
- 1 cup sugar
- 1 teaspoon baking powder
- 1 pinch salt
- ¼ cup margarine, melted
- 1 teaspoon vanilla
- 1 egg
- ½ cup soymilk
- 1 cup firm tofu, grated

Preheat the oven to 350°F. Mix all of the dry ingredients together in a large bowl. Stir in the margarine, vanilla, egg, soymilk, and tofu. When the batter is thoroughly mixed, place in a well greased bread pan. Bake for 45 minutes or until a knife inserted in the middle comes out clean.

Makes one loaf (8 slices)

Per slice: Calories: 229, Protein: 5 gm., Fat: 7 gm., Carbohydrates: 35 gm.

Torta de Naranja

(orange cake)

- 1¾ cups unbleached white flour
- ¼ cup soy flour
- 1 teaspoon baking powder
- ½ cup margarine
- 1 cup sugar
- 1 teaspoon vanilla
- juice of 2 medium oranges
- 1 teaspoon cinnamon

Preheat the oven to 375°F. In a medium bowl, mix the flours and baking powder. In a small sauce pan, melt the margarine, add the sugar, vanilla, orange juice, and cinnamon and add to the flour mixture, stirring until well blended. Pour the mixture in a lightly oiled, 8" x 9" cake pan, and bake for 30 minutes.

Makes 12 pieces

Per piece: Calories: 201, Protein: 3 gm., Fat: 7 gm., Carbohydrates: 29 gm.

Africa

Most of the recipes in this section are from two very different countries where Plenty technicians have worked—Liberia, on the northwest coast, and Lesotho, a tiny southern republic surrounded by South Africa.

People living in rural Lesotho rely on milimeal (a grain), corn, white flour, potatoes, cabbage, tomatoes, and onions for the bulk of their diet, as well as, to a lesser degree, peaches, apricots, and prickly pear fruit. Coconuts, cassava, yams, mangos, pineapples, and vegetable greens are common in the more tropical Liberian diet.

We hope you will enjoy preparing and serving some of the simple, yet tasty, recipes from these countries included in this section.

Soy Demonstrations in Lesotho, Africa

In the spring of 1984, I went on my first overseas assignment, representing

Plenty in the country of Lesotho, Africa. Unlike many parts of Africa, Lesotho does not have a lush, tropical climate. It's located in the mountains, very dry for most of the year, and cold with some snowfall during the winter months. Its terrain reminded me of areas in the southwest U.S. and northern Mexico.

Plenty was working with villagers in Lesotho's Quthing Valley, helping improve agricultural production, planting trees, establishing village water systems, designing a rural health care project, assisting a foot-bridge building project, and introducing the use of soybeans into a diet that for many lacked sufficient protein. The staff consisted of local Basotho along with people from South Africa, Mozambique, Argentina, Spain, Canada, and the United States, who were giving technical and administrative support.

It was my job to work with the Lesotho staff to establish an educational program for people interested in learning soybean processing methods, as well as to design and outfit the soybean processing education center at our project headquarters.

In contrast to the western sleeping patterns I was used to, when the sun sets, people go to bed in rural Lesotho. At night, the brilliance of the stars was only slightly dimmed by our solar-lit, small roundhouses at Motsemocha, the village-technology educational center

we were helping to establish. While the villagers surrounding us slept, we foreigners would stay awake, finding ways to entertain ourselves. Solar electrical systems powered everything from reading lights to video machines, and a generator powered the small electric amplifiers for guitars and key boards that some of our staff had brought with them.

Every morning I would wake up in the fresh mountain air to sounds of men and women singing as they worked threshing milimeal grain on tarps with wooden poles, filling sacks, and carrying these to their homes. Dragging myself from bed into the open air a passerby would offer *"Dume la dade."* (Good morning sir.), *"O peele juah?"* (How are things?) The Basotho people have an incredible sense of humor, and when these mountain people speak it sounds as though they are singing.

For over two years prior to my arrival, Basotho women and Plenty volunteers had been telling people in surrounding villages about the nutritional qualities of soybeans and showing them how the beans could be used in traditional meals. These local women and volunteers would be up early in the morning cleaning the soybeans that would be used that day. The beans would be cooked over open fires and made into fresh soymilk and tofu. Everyone attending the daily processing demonstration would be given a glass of soymilk with a little added sugar. The remaining milk would be made into tofu, and then stir fried with onions, tomatoes, salt, and black pepper in a little oil. The leftover pulp (okara) was included in baked or fried foods.

The people I met loved these foods, and they always showed great appreciation for the time the women had taken to come and visit their village, bringing knowledge of this new food source. I will never forget the smiles on the children's faces and eruptions of laughter during the singing and dancing that inevitably followed a soybean processing demonstration in the mountains of the Quthing Valley in Lesotho.

Chuck Haren

Soy Promotion at Imani House, Liberia

At the same time the world was focused on the Gulf War, civil conflicts were erupting in the west African nation of Liberia. Thousands of families were uprooted, crops were destroyed and the incidence of malnutrition rose dramatically. Two African-Americans who had been living in Liberia for several years, together with some Liberian friends, established an organization they called Imani House to provide food, medical care, and educational support for orphaned children and others suffering due to the war.

In April of 1992, I went to Liberia to assist Imani House soy programs. We first worked with the children, cooks, teachers, and caretakers at the Imani House children's home, showing everyone how to use soybeans in their daily meals. At the market in Monrovia, we were lucky to have found a few spices and seasonings before the demonstration, as foods and spices common to the Liberian diet were almost nonexistent during the war. As we prepared the ingredients, all the children and adults swarmed around us, vying for a chance to help crush the soybeans with a huge mortar and pestle, or to stir the soymilk cooking in large pots over the open fire. Despite our limited choice of ingredients, everyone loved the hot soymilk with a little sugar and cinnamon, the fritters made from okara, white flour, curry, onions, garlic, pepper, and salt, and the crunchy soy nuts we showed them how to make.

In the village of Duason, Imani House was just starting to help farming families reestablish crops of cassava and vegetable greens that had been destroyed during the war. We talked to farmers about how soybeans could be included in their traditional agricultural cycles. We also conducted a daylong soyfoods cooking program attended by many families from the village, technicians working with the United Nations Food and Agriculture Organization, a nutritionist, and home economists working with another international nongovernmental organization. People were skeptical at first, and then delighted to see the number of delicious foods that could be made from a small amount of these strange, new beans.

We also visited many of the women preparing meals for children at several recently reopened schools. In most cases, these were the only full meals the children were getting. Many of the school feeding centers had received soybeans from the United Nations, but the cooks didn't know how to prepare them.

I was amazed by the fortitude of the Liberian women we met on these visits! Despite the tragedies of the war surrounding them and the daily struggle to feed all the children in their care with few resources, these women were extremely gracious in receiving us. They were very eager to learn more about methods of using soybeans.

Today the staff of Imani House continues to help some of the children hardest hit by Liberia's civil war, as well as teaching educators, farmers, families, and micro-entrepreneurs about the valuable role soybeans can play in helping Liberia provide for its nutritional needs.

Chuck Haren

Main Dishes

Mozambican Piripiri

You can prepare this zestful dinner course in 15 minutes.

½ lb firm tofu
1 tablespoon oil
2 small hot peppers, diced
1 large sweet yellow pepper, chopped
2 cloves garlic, diced
juice of 1 fresh lime or lemon
2 tablespoons soy sauce

Cut the tofu into 2 x 2 x ¼-inch thick slices. Heat the oil in a medium skillet. When the oil is very hot, add the tofu, and fry until the bottom is golden brown. Flip the tofu and add the peppers, garlic, lime or lemon juice, and soy sauce. Simmer on medium heat until the tofu is golden brown on the other side. Serve with rice or baked potatoes and your favorite green vegetable.

Serves 3

Per serving: Calories: 118, Protein: 7 gm., Fat: 8 gm., Carbohydrates: 5 gm.

Tofu Yam Balls

An excellent appetizer before a larger meal.

4 cups yams or white potatoes, boiled and mashed
3 cups tofu, finely crumbled
1 small onion, chopped
1 tablespoon peanut oil
1 teaspoon black pepper
1 teaspoon salt
1½ cups unbleached white flour
vegetable oil for frying

In a medium bowl, mix all of the ingredients together, except the flour and frying oil. Stir in 1 cup of flour, and mix well. Form the mixture into small balls. Roll in the remaining flour, and deep fry in very hot oil until golden brown.

Serves 6

Per serving: Calories: 324, Protein: 13 gm., Fat: 8 gm., Carbohydrates: 50 gm.

Coconut Rice with Tempeh

Here's a wonderful dish with a rich, savory flavor!

¼ lb tempeh, cut in small cubes
1 tablespoon oil
1 medium onion, chopped
1 teaspoon oil
1 cup uncooked rice
1 cup coconut milk
2 medium tomatoes, chopped
1 teaspoon dry thyme
1 teaspoon salt
¾ cup water

In a medium frying pan, lightly brown the tempeh in 1 tablespoon of oil. Add the onion to the tempeh, and stir fry for 3 minutes, adding a little water if necessary to prevent sticking. Heat 1 teaspoon of oil in a small skillet, add the rice, and toast on medium-low heat for about 7 minutes, stirring often. Add the toasted rice to the tempeh and onions, and cook over medium-low heat. Stir in the coconut milk, tomatoes, thyme, salt, and water. Cover the pan and simmer for 15 to 20 minutes or until all of the liquid is absorbed. Remove from the heat, and serve with cooked greens or sweet corn.

Serves 6

Per serving: Calories: 222, Protein: 7 gm., Fat: 5 gm., Carbohydrates: 36 gm.

West African Wara Scramble

½ lb tofu
2 cups water, lightly salted
1 cup water
2 teaspoons salt
2 teaspoons sugar
1½ cups fresh green beans, cut in small pieces
1 tablespoon oil
1 large tomato, chopped
1 small summer squash, chopped
1 medium onion, chopped
½ teaspoon dry thyme
2 tablespoons soy sauce
1 tablespoon nutritional yeast

Crumble the tofu in a small saucepan, add the lightly salted water, and bring to a boil. Drain in a colander lined with cheesecloth. Using the same saucepan, combine the water with half the salt and sugar, add the green beans, and boil until tender. Heat the oil in a large frying pan, and sauté the tomato, squash, and onion. Add the green beans, the liquid remaining in the saucepan, and the tofu. Season with the remaining salt and sugar, the thyme, soy sauce, and nutritional yeast. Cook on low heat for 5 minutes, stirring constantly.

Serves 6

Per serving: Calories: 88, Protein: 5 gm., Fat: 4 gm., Carbohydrates: 8 gm.

Steamed Corn and Tofu

This meal can only be prepared when fresh green field corn is in season.

6 ears of fresh green field corn (page 11)
1 cup firm tofu, crumbled
1 small onion, finely chopped
1 small red pepper, finely chopped
1 teaspoon salt
½ teaspoon black pepper
1 tablespoon margarine
16 dry or green corn husks

Scrape the corn kernels from the cob. Grind the corn in a grain mill, or blend into a paste using a blender, adding a little water if necessary. Place the corn in a large mixing bowl, and add the tofu. Stir in the onion, red pepper, salt, black pepper, and margarine. To prepare the corn husks: First open and rinse the husks. If using dry corn husks, place them in cool water for 3 minutes. Remove the leaves from the water and place 2 together. Fill with 3 tablespoons of the mixture. Fold one side, then the other over the top of the mixture. Fold the remaining top and bottom across the center to form a small packet. Repeat this process until all of the mixture is used. Stack them on a perforated rack or colander inside a large pot with 4 cups of boiling water, cover, and steam for 50 minutes. Make sure they are above the boiling water, and that they are stacked to allow the steam to circulate around them. Serve with vegetables or soup.

Serves 6

Per serving: Calories: 209, Protein: 10 gm., Fat: 5 gm., Carbohydrates: 31 gm.

Soy Moinmoin

This recipe and the Steamed Corn and Tofu recipe (page 85) make dishes similar in texture to the tamales in the Central American section but have a much different flavor.

¾ cup soybeans
½ cup black-eyed peas
½ cup dry field corn
6 cups water
1 teaspoon salt
½ teaspoon fennel seed
½ teaspoon dry thyme
1 medium onion, chopped
1 tablespoon black pepper
¼ cup oil
16 corn, banana, or grape leaves

Rinse the soybeans, black-eyed peas, and corn. In a large pot, combine the soybeans, black-eyed peas, corn, water, and salt, and boil for 1 hour. After thirty minutes, add more water if needed, along with the fennel seed and thyme. After 1 hour, remove from the heat, and drain. Grind the soybeans, black-eyed peas, corn and onion into a paste with a grain mill, blender, or mortar and pestle. Stir in the black pepper and oil. Wrap 2 large spoonfuls of this mixture in 2 washed leaves. Fold one side, then the other over the top of the mixture. Fold the remaining top and bottom across the center to form a small packet. Repeat this process until all of the mixture is used. Stack them on a perforated rack or colander inside a large pot with 4 cups of boiling water, cover, and steam for 50 minutes. Make sure they are above the boiling water, and that they are stacked to allow the steam to circulate around them. Check the water level periodically, and add more if necessary. These are good served with steamed vegetables or soup.

Serves 6 to 8

Per serving: Calories: 264, Protein: 12 gm., Fat: 11 gm., Carbohydrates: 27 gm.

Side Dishes

Tofu and Pea Puree

A great appetizer or chip dip.

2 cups tofu, cubed
1 cup cooked pigeon peas (page13)
½ cup coconut milk
1 tablespoon lime juice
1 tablespoon soy sauce
½ teaspoon salt

Put all of the ingredients in a blender, and blend on low speed until thick and smooth. (You will have to periodically stop the blender, and push the ingredients down with a rubber scraper or spoon.) You can also place all of the ingredients in a bowl, mash, and stir until smooth. Serve with crackers, chips, or your favorite breads.

Makes approximately 3 cups

Per 2 tablespoons: Calories: 37, Protein: 2 gm., Fat: 2 gm., Carbohydrates: 2 gm.

Soyogi

This protein-packed, hot breakfast cereal has a great nutty flavor and delivers a charge of nutrients for you and your children.

½ cup soy flour
1½ cups corn meal
3½ cups soymilk
1 teaspoon ground cinnamon
1 teaspoon vanilla

In a large skillet, lightly toast the soy flour and corn meal together, stirring often to prevent burning. In a medium saucepan, bring the soymilk to a gentle boil, stirring often to prevent sticking. Add the cinnamon and vanilla. Lower the heat and add the toasted soy flour and corn meal a little at a time, stirring with a wire whisk to prevent lumps. Continue cooking and stirring the cereal for 2 or 3 minutes. Soyogi should be served when hot and creamy. Add honey or other sweetener to taste.

Serves 4 to 6

Soyakara

One of the most common fast foods in West Africa and the Caribbean.

1 cup firm tofu, grated
1 cup cooked garbanzo beans, mashed
¾ cup whole wheat flour
½ teaspoon garlic powder
3 tablespoons onion, finely chopped
1 teaspoon salt
½ teaspoon black pepper
oil for frying

With a clean towel or fine strainer, squeeze the excess water from the tofu. Thoroughly mix the tofu with the garbanzo paste, then add the flour, garlic, onion, salt, and black pepper. Make 1½-inch balls. Deep fry in hot oil until golden brown. Serve as snacks or with gravy over rice.

Serves 4

Per serving: Calories: 192, Protein: 10 gm., Fat: 4 gm., Carbohydrates: 28 gm.

Eba Soy

A very nutritious and filling side dish from West Africa. It's great for those days when you need something solid with a good bowl of soup.

½ cup soy flour
3 cups water
1½ cups cassava flour (page 10)

Add the soy flour to boiling water and stir to make a paste. Remove from the heat and mix in the cassava flour. Stir the mixture until firm. Slice or spoon onto small plates, and serve with vegetable soup.

Serves 4 to 6

Per serving: Calories: 210, Protein: 4 gm., Fat: 2 gm., Carbohydrates: 43 gm.

Soups and Stews

Pigeon Pea Stew

Pigeon peas are one of the most common legumes eaten in many parts of Africa and the Caribbean.

1 cup dry pigeon peas (page 13) or small red beans
3 cups water for soaking
4 cups water
1 cup tofu or tempeh, cubed
2 tablespoons oil
1 small onion, chopped
2 cups cooked hominy
1 hot pepper, diced
1 teaspoon salt
1 tablespoon soy sauce
1 tablespoon nutritional yeast

Soak the pigeon peas or red beans in 3 cups water for 1 to 3 hours, and drain. Bring 4 cups water to a boil for about 1 hour until they are soft. In a small skillet, sauté the tofu or tempeh in the oil until brown on all sides, and add the onion. Add the hominy to the pigeon peas, and cook for 5 minutes. Add the tofu or tempeh and onions, hot pepper, salt, soy sauce, and nutritional yeast, and cook for 10 more minutes. Serve with corn, cassava, or other breads, and a salad.

Serves 6

Per serving: Calories: 193, Protein: 9 gm., Fat: 6 gm., Carbohydrates: 24 gm.

South African Sweet Potato and Tempeh Stew

We never seem to have enough of this for our children when it is served.

2 lbs sweet potatoes, peeled and
    chopped
2 cups water
2 tablespoons oil
½ lb tempeh, cut in strips
¼ cup brown sugar
2 tablespoons margarine, melted
1 tablespoon ground cinnamon
1 tablespoon corn meal
1 teaspoon salt

In a medium pot, cook the sweet potatoes in 1 cup water until they start to become soft, and remove from heat. In a large frying pan, heat the oil and fry the tempeh on both sides until brown and crisp. In a small bowl, mix the brown sugar, margarine, cinnamon, corn meal, and salt. In a second medium-sized pot, add the remaining cup of water, half of the sweet potatoes, and half of the tempeh. Spread half of the brown sugar, margarine, cinnamon, corn meal, and salt on top. Next, add the remaining sweet potatoes and tempeh, then add the remaining brown sugar, margarine, cinnamon, corn meal, and salt. Simmer for 15 minutes. This is delicious with hot corn bread.

Serves 4

Per serving: Calories: 529, Protein: 12 gm., Fat: 16 gm., Carbohydrates: 83 gm.

Pepper Soup With Plantain

This flavorful soup is another Nigerian adaptation for the pepper lovers in your family.

3 cups water
1 large carrot, chopped
3 medium tomatoes, chopped
1 teaspoon salt
½ lb tofu
1 tablespoon oil
1 medium onion, chopped
1 medium green pepper, chopped
2 sweet yellow peppers, chopped
1 medium sweet red pepper, chopped
1 small fresh hot pepper, minced
2 tablespoons soy sauce
⅓ teaspoon dry thyme
⅓ teaspoon dry parsley
2 half ripe plantains (yellowish-green in color)
2 teaspoons oil

In a large pot, combine the water, carrot, tomatoes, and salt. Bring to a boil, lower the heat, and simmer slowly. Cut the tofu into slices about 2 inches long, 1 inch wide, and ¼ inch thick. In a medium skillet, heat 1 tablespoon oil. When the oil is hot, lightly brown the tofu on one side, flip, add the onions, cover, and sauté for 2 minutes. Stir in all of the peppers with the tofu and onion, cover, and cook for 4 more minutes. Add the soy sauce. When the peppers are beginning to soften, add the tofu, onion, and pepper mixture to the pot with the carrots and tomatoes. Add the thyme and parsley, and simmer while preparing the plantains. Peel and slice the plantains into ¼-inch thick rounds. In the same skillet used for the tofu, fry the plantains in 2 teaspoons oil until crispy on both sides. Drain on a plate covered with a paper towel, and serve with the soup.

Serves 4 to 6

Per serving: Calories: 207, Protein: 6 gm., Fat: 7 gm., Carbohydrates: 30 gm.

Tempeh and Ground Nut Stew

A couple of good helpings of this stew will leave you full for three meals.

2 tablespoons oil
½ lb tempeh, cut in small cubes
½ cup peanut butter
3 to 4 cups water
2 medium tomatoes, chopped
1 medium onion, chopped
1 chili pepper, diced
1 medium bell pepper, chopped
1 teaspoon salt

In a medium skillet, heat the oil and brown the tempeh on all sides. While the tempeh is frying, heat the peanut butter and water in a medium saucepan, stirring frequently to prevent burning. When the peanut butter is dissolved, add the tomatoes, and simmer, stirring often. When the tempeh is golden on one side, flip, stir in the onion, chili pepper, and bell pepper, and cook until soft. Add this and all of the remaining ingredients to the peanut and tomato stew. Add the salt and simmer for 10 to 15 minutes. Serve with crackers and rice or baked potatoes.

Serves 4 to 6

Per serving: Calories: 313, Protein: 14 gm., Fat: 20 gm., Carbohydrates: 18 gm.

Quthing Valley Bean Soup

The people in the Quthing Valley of Lesotho do not have the variety of vegetables, seasonings, and spices we are used to in North America, but this soup has a light, balanced flavor that is great anytime.

1 cup soybeans
3 cups water for soaking
6 cups water
½ small onion, chopped
1 medium tomato, chopped
1 clove garlic, crushed
1 teaspoon oil
1 teaspoon dry thyme
1 teaspoon salt

Rinse the soybeans and soak in 3 cups water for 7 to 10 hours (maximum). Drain and rinse the soybeans, and grind coarsely in a grain mill. Bring the 6 cups of water to boil in a large pot. Add the ground soybeans and simmer. In a medium skillet, sauté the onion, tomato, and garlic in the oil for 5 minutes. Add the sautéed vegetables, thyme, and salt to the soybeans. Let the soup simmer for 25 minutes, adding a little more water if needed.

Serves 4 to 5

Per serving: Calories: 86, Protein: 6 gm., Fat: 4 gm., Carbohydrates: 6 gm.

Yams and Wara Stew

This stew is adapted from a traditional Nigerian recipe. In Nigeria tofu is called "wara."

1 lb yams or white potatoes, cut into pieces
3 medium tomatoes, chopped
1 medium bell pepper, chopped
1 medium onion, chopped
2 cloves garlic, chopped
2 teaspoons oil
½ lb firm tofu, cubed
1 cup cooked black-eyed peas
1 teaspoon salt or 1 tablespoon soy sauce

In a medium pot, boil the yams or potatoes until soft. Grind or blend together the tomatoes, bell pepper, onion, and garlic. Heat the oil in a medium frying pan, add the tofu, and brown on all sides. Add all of the vegetables to the tofu, and simmer for 3 minutes. Add the black-eyed peas and salt or soy sauce, and cook for 10 more minutes. This stew is delicious with cassava or corn bread.

Serves 4

Per serving: Calories: 247, Protein: 9 gm., Fat: 5 gm., Carbohydrates: 40 gm.

Desserts

Liberian Pineapple Coconut Pie

We hear only one phrase from our friends who try this. "More please!"

2½ cups pineapple, crushed
½ cup coconut, shredded
½ cup tofu, grated
½ cup sugar
1 tablespoon lime juice
1 tablespoon margarine, melted

pie crust:
½ teaspoon salt
1¾ cups flour
¼ cup margarine or oil
6 to 8 tablespoons water

With a strainer, squeeze the excess juice from the crushed pineapple. In a medium mixing bowl, stir together the pineapple, coconut, tofu, sugar, lime juice, and margarine. Preheat the oven to 375°F. To make the pie crust: Mix the salt and flour, then add the oil and enough water to make a smooth dough. Divide into 2 pieces and roll out on a floured surface or between 2 sheets of waxed paper. Line an 8-inch pie pan with half of the dough, and bake for 10 minutes. Remove the crust from the oven, pour in the pie mix, and cover with the second pie dough, and seal the edges. Bake until the pie crust is brown, approximately 30 minutes.

Makes 8 pieces

Per piece: Calories: 354, Protein: 5 gm., Fat: 16 gm., Carbohydrates: 44 gm.

Cassava Banana Cookies

You will find the texture of these cookies unique and enjoyable.

1 cup unbleached white flour
½ cup cassava flour (page 10)
½ cup soy flour
¾ cup sugar
3 teaspoons baking powder
1 teaspoon salt
½ cup margarine, melted
1 ripe banana, mashed
1 cup milk

Preheat the oven to 325°F. Mix all of the dry ingredients together in a medium bowl. Stir in the margarine and add the banana and milk. Mix to form a nice light dough. Drop large tablespoons of the dough onto oiled cookie sheets, and bake for about 25 minutes, or until the bottoms are crispy.

Makes 24 cookies

Per cookie: Calories: 102, Protein: 2 gm., Fat: 5 gm., Carbohydrates: 14 gm.

Soy Corn Crunch

There isn't a culture in the world that doesn't love sweets. So why not make them better for you by adding high protein corn and soy?

2 cups cornmeal
½ cup full-fat soy flour (page 11)
4 tablespoons sugar
hot water
oil for frying

Mix the corn and soy flours together with the sugar. Add just enough hot water to make a smooth but stiff dough. Let set for 20 minutes. Take the dough a little at a time, and roll it with the palm of both hands, and pat into a thin circle. Heat the oil and fry until brown. Drain on paper towels.

Serves 4

Per serving: Calories: 358, Protein: 11 gm., Fat: 4 gm., Carbohydrates: 70 gm.

Motsemocha Peach Cobbler

Peaches and apricots are the most common fruits grown in Lesotho. Enjoy this variation of a recipe that some of our volunteers have used while working in the highlands of the Quthing Valley.

6 large peaches
3 tablespoons margarine
3 tablespoons sugar
1 teaspoon cinnamon

Batter:

1½ cups unbleached white flour
⅓ cup sugar
1½ teaspoons baking powder
¼ cup oil
1 cup soymilk
1 teaspoon vanilla

Wash, peel, remove the seeds, and cut the peaches into slices. Heat the margarine in a large skillet, add the peaches, and cook on low heat for about 5 minutes. Add 3 tablespoons sugar and cinnamon and cook 10 more minutes, and remove from the heat. Preheat the oven to 350°F. To make the batter: Combine the flour, ⅓ cup sugar, and baking powder, stir together, and add the oil, soymilk, and vanilla, and mix well. Pour a layer of the batter in an oiled, medium baking pan. Cover with a layer of peaches, and pour the remaining batter over the peaches. Bake for about 25 minutes.

Serves 8

Per serving: Calories: 269, Protein: 4 gm., Fat: 9 gm., Carbohydrates: 31 gm.

Papaya Pudding

What can we say about papaya? It has a subtle, rich but not overly sweet flavor and a silky texture. Enjoy.

- **2 cups papaya, chopped**
- **1 cup soymilk**
- **1 tablespoon lime juice**
- **1 teaspoon vanilla**
- **½ cup sugar**
- **¼ cup corn starch**
- **¼ teaspoon salt**
- **2 tablespoons margarine**

In a blender, combine the papaya, soymilk, lime juice, and vanilla, and blend until smooth. In a medium saucepan, stir together the sugar, corn starch, and salt. Pour in the papaya mix, and simmer on low heat for 5 minutes. Remove from the heat, stir in the margarine, pour into cups, and chill.

Makes 3 cups

Per ½ cup: Calories: 135, Protein: 1 gm., Fat: 5 gm., Carbohydrates: 22 gm.

Rum Raisin Ice Cream

This is the favorite ice cream of our African and Caribbean friends.

- **3 cups soymilk**
- **1 cup raisins**
- **1 cup sugar**
- **⅓ cup oil**
- **¼ cup powdered soymilk**
- **1 double shot glass of rum**
- **1 teaspoon carrageenan (sea moss)**
  (page 13) (use as directed)
- **½ teaspoon vanilla**
- **1 teaspoon ground nutmeg**
- **¼ teaspoon salt**

Blend all of the ingredients together in a blender. Follow the directions for freezing from your electric or hand crank ice cream machine.

Makes 4½ cups

Per cup: Calories: 470, Protein: 4 gm., Fat: 17 gm., Carbohydrates: 66 gm.

Sri Lanka

Sri Lanka is an island country off the southeast coast of India populated by more than 17 million people. It is a land of herbs and spices, all of which are used in abundance in traditional cooking. Curry leaves, cloves, ginger, allspice, nutmeg, cinnamon, coriander, capsicum, turmeric, chilies, garlic, onions, leeks, mint, and lemon grass are only some of the many flavors typically added to daily meals. Rice, yogurt, and sweet chutneys are often served on the side to help quell the eye-watering heat resulting from these intensely curried dishes. The foods included in this section are as common to the people of Sri Lanka as sweet corn, or pumpkin pie are to most of us in North America.

Soy Utilization in Sri Lanka

While employed with Plenty Canada the late 1980s, I made three trips to Sri Lanka. We had been asked to work with local groups and demonstrate how small-business-scale, soybean processing methods could be successfully adapted to local conditions.

Many Sri Lankans were interested in producing and marketing more of the country's basic food needs. In the 1970s and into the early 1980s, major gains had been made in adapting soybean cultivation to local agricultural practices. Farmers had actually begun producing more soybeans than were being consumed. The large factories which had been set up to process soybeans into oil, animal feed, textured vegetable protein, and flour had many technical and management problems. In addition, they were not producing affordable products acceptable to local cultural tastes.

Beginning in 1987, Plenty Canada's staff concentrated on small-scale soy utilization projects. They taught many small entrepreneurs, in and around the cities of Kandy and Colombo, how to incorporate soy products into the foods they were marketing. Many Sri Lankans are vegetarians and have been eager to add soybeans to their traditional foods. Their great taste, low cost, high nutritional value, ease of preparation, and adaptability to familiar food forms and flavors have made soybean products popular in Sri Lanka.

Chuck Haren

Breads

Roti

These are great served with curries. If you don't have time to make your own, you can buy them at East Indian or health food stores.

1½ cups water
¼ cup cracked, dehulled soybeans
   (page 16)
¾ cup whole wheat flour
3 tablespoons fresh coconut, finely
   grated
2 tablespoons onion, finely grated
1 tablespoon chili pepper
1 teaspoon salt

Bring the water to a boil, add the cracked dehulled soybeans, cover, and simmer for 20 minutes, adding a little more water if needed. Drain the soybeans, and grind in a grain mill to a fine paste. Mix the whole wheat flour with the soybean paste, and add the coconut, onion, chili pepper, and salt. Add a little water, if needed, to make a nice soft dough. Cut or tear into 6 to 8 pieces, and roll into balls. Flatten very thin by hand or with a rolling pin. Cook on a lightly oiled, small frying pan until light brown on both sides.

Makes 6 to 8 rotis

Per roti: Calories: 105, Protein: 4 gm., Fat: 5 gm., Carbohydrates: 11 gm.

Chapati

1½ cups whole wheat flour
½ cup soy flour
½ teaspoon salt
1 cup water

In a medium bowl, combine the whole wheat flour, soy flour, and salt, and mix well. Add enough water to make a soft dough, and knead until smooth. Cover the bowl with a clean towel, and let set at room temperature for 15 minutes. Knead again for 3 minutes, then divide the dough into 10 to 12 equal portions, and shape into round balls. Roll out each ball into a flat 5-inch circle, adding a little flour to each side while rolling to prevent sticking. Heat a medium frying pan, and cook each chapati for 1 minute on each side or until firm to the touch. Place each chapati on a wire rack or hold over the flame of a gas or electric burner on medium high heat for a few seconds until the bread puffs. Be careful not to burn yourself or the chapati! Serve with warm margarine or butter. Chapatis are also good with any curry or dal.

Serves 6

Per serving: Calories: 142, Protein: 7 gm., Fat: 2 gm., Carbohydrates: 23 gm.

Appetizers

Sambol

1½ cups water
¼ cup cracked, dehulled soybeans
  (page 16)
½ fresh coconut, finely grated
2 small dry hot peppers, finely ground
  or grated
2 small red onions, diced or finely
  grated
1 tablespoon lime juice
½ teaspoon salt

Bring the water to a boil, add the cracked dehulled soybeans, cover, and simmer for 20 minutes, adding a little more water if needed. Preheat the oven to 350°F. Drain the soybeans, and spread them on a clean cloth or paper towel to dry. Dry-roast the soybean pieces on a cookie sheet in the oven until crisp and golden brown. Stir occasionally when baking to prevent sticking. With a grain mill, grind the dry roasted soybean pieces to a flour. In a medium bowl, mix the ground soybean flour, coconut, hot peppers, onions, lime juice, and salt. This is a good appetizer served alongside curry and rice dishes.

Serves 8

Per serving: Calories: 118, Protein: 3 gm., Fat: 10 gm., Carbohydrates: 5 gm.

Coconut Chutney

1 fresh coconut, grated
6 green chilies, diced
1 teaspoon mustard seeds
1 tablespoon oil
1½ cups water
¼ cup soybeans
1 small sized ball of tamarind (page 14)
salt to taste

Sauté the coconut, green chilies, and mustard seeds in the oil. Bring the water to a boil, add the soybeans, cover, and simmer for 20 minutes adding a little more water if needed. Preheat the oven to 350°F. Drain the soybeans and spread the blanched beans on a clean cloth or paper towel to dry. Dry-roast the soybeans on a cookie sheet in the oven until crisp and golden brown. Stir occasionally when baking to prevent sticking. Combine the roasted soybeans and coconut mixture, and mix thoroughly. Add the tamarind and salt, and grind the mixture in a hand mill to a fine paste. Mix with enough boiling water to make a chutney of the desired consistency. Serve with any meal.

Makes 3 cups

Per tablespoon: Calories: 55, Protein: 1 gm., Fat: 4 gm., Carbohydrates: 2 gm.

Tofu Pittu

This is a delightful, mild-flavored appetizer that compliments spicy, East Indian food.

½ cup firm tofu, grated
½ cup unbleached white or rice flour
½ cup green leafy vegetables, chopped
½ cup fresh coconut, grated
1 teaspoon salt

Mix the tofu, flour, greens, and coconut together thoroughly. Add the salt and a little water if necessary. Steam either in a pittu-bamboo or string hopper steamer (page 9) for 15 minutes.

Serves 4

Per serving: Calories: 266, Protein: 6 gm., Fat: 18 gm., Carbohydrates: 18 gm.

Waddai

2 cups water
1 cup cracked, dehulled soybeans
    (page 16)
2 tablespoons onions, diced
1 tablespoon green chili peppers, diced
2 tablespoons fresh gingerroot, grated
1 teaspoon salt
1 teaspoon curry powder
1 teaspoon chili powder
3 tablespoons unbleached white flour
oil for deep frying

In a medium saucepan, bring the water to a boil, and drop in the soybeans. Boil for 20 minutes, and drain. Divide the blanched beans in half. Grind 1 portion to a fine paste in a grain mill, then mix with the unground soybeans in a medium size bowl. In a small bowl, combine the onions, green chilli peppers, gingerroot, salt, curry, and chili powder. Add the combined seasonings to the soybean paste, and mix well, without adding any water. Mix in the flour. Make small balls about ½ inch thick. (It helps to wet your hands when shaping each waddai.) Deep fry in very hot oil until golden brown on both sides. Serve with steamed vegetables and rice.

Makes 12 waddai

Per waddai: Calories: 32, Protein: 2 gm., Fat: 1 gm., Carbohydrates: 3 gm.

Potato Tofu Cutlets

1 cup firm tofu, grated
2 medium potatoes, peeled and diced
1 teaspoon black pepper
½ teaspoon chili powder
½ teaspoon curry powder
1 tablespoon lime juice
1 teaspoon salt
3 tablespoons onions, diced
2 tablespoons green chilies, diced
½-inch piece fresh gingerroot, diced
½ cup unbleached white flour
⅔ cup water
1 cup fine bread crumbs
oil for frying

Put the grated tofu in a clean cloth, and squeeze out the excess water before measuring. Boil potatoes until soft, drain, and mash. Mix the tofu and mashed potatoes with the black pepper, chili powder, curry, lime juice, salt, onions, green chilies, ginger, and 4 tablespoons of flour. Combine the remaining flour and the water to make a thin batter. Roll the cutlet dough into small balls, dip in the batter, and roll in the bread crumbs. Deep fry in hot oil until golden brown. These are a great snack food.

Makes about 20 cutlets

Per cutlet: Calories: 62, Protein: 2 gm., Fat: 0 gm., Carbohydrates: 11 gm.

Tempeh Omelet

¼ lb tempeh
1 tablespoon onion, diced
2 green chilies, chopped
1 small tomato, diced
1 teaspoon curry powder
2 tablespoons unbleached white flour
½ teaspoon black pepper
½ teaspoon salt
⅓ cup water
1 tablespoon oil

Cut the tempeh into thin slices, steam for 15 minutes, drain, and mash. In a medium bowl, mix the tempeh with the onion, chilies, tomato, and curry powder. Stir in the flour, black pepper, salt, and water, and mix thoroughly. Heat the oil in a medium frying pan. Pour in the omelet mixture, and cook both sides on medium heat until golden brown. Let the first side of the omelet cook enough so that it will turn it over in one piece. Serve with toast or chapatis.

Serves 2 to 3

Per serving: Calories: 185, Protein: 9 gm., Fat: 8 gm., Carbohydrates: 18 gm

Spiced Tempeh with Yogurt

2 tablespoons oil
½ teaspoon mustard seeds
1 tablespoon onion, diced
4 cloves garlic, crushed
2 thin slices fresh gingerroot, crushed
4 fresh green chilies, diced
¼ lb tempeh, cut into 2-inch strips
4 tablespoons plain yogurt
½ cup water
1 teaspoon salt

In a medium frying pan heat the oil and sauté the mustard seeds, onion, garlic, gingerroot, and green chilies. Add the tempeh and sauté for 10 minutes, stirring several times until the tempeh is cooked on both sides. Stir in the yogurt, water, and salt. Cover, and simmer for 10 more minutes. Serve with rice, boiled potatoes, or pasta.

Serves 3

Per serving: Calories: 196, Protein: 8 gm., Fat: 12 gm., Carbohydrates: 13 gm.

Tofu Snack

2 tablespoons soy sauce
2 teaspoons curry powder
2 teaspoons chili powder
1 teaspoon salt
1 cup water
½ lb firm tofu, cut into 1-inch cubes
oil for frying

In a medium bowl, mix the soy sauce, curry, chili powder, salt, and water. Add the tofu and marinate for 30 minutes. Drain and deep fry in a medium saucepan until golden brown. Serve hot with sweet and sour sauce.

Serves 3 to 4

Per serving: Calories: 55, Protein: 5 gm., Fat: 3 gm., Carbohydrates: 2 gm.

Sri Lankan Noodle Soup

6 cups water
1 medium potato, diced
1 medium carrot, diced
2 stalks celery, chopped
1 medium tomato, diced
1 teaspoon salt
1 teaspoon black pepper
1 teaspoon curry powder
¼ lb tofu, cubed
½ cup corn flour
3 tablespoons oil
1 medium Bombay onion, chopped
8 ounces uncooked pasta

In a large pot, bring the water to a boil, add the potato and carrot, return to a boil, lower the heat, and simmer for 5 minutes. Add the celery, tomato, salt, black pepper, and curry. While the soup is cooking, coat the tofu cubes with the corn flour. Heat the oil and fry until golden, stirring often in a medium frying pan. Add the onion and cook until soft and lightly browned. Add the tofu and onion mix to the soup. Add your favorite noodles and simmer for another 10 minutes or until the noodles are soft.

Serves 6 to 8

Per serving: Calories: 170, Protein: 4 gm., Fat: 7 gm., Carbohydrates: 23 gm.

Curries

Potato Soymilk Curry

2 medium potatoes, cut in small cubes
1 tablespoon onion, diced
1 teaspoon mustard seed
3 tablespoons oil
1 teaspoon turmeric
2 teaspoons curry powder
2 teaspoons chili powder
1 teaspoon salt
2 cups soymilk
1 tablespoon lime juice

Sauté the potatoes, onions, and mustard seeds in the oil. Add the turmeric, curry, chili powder, and salt, and mix well. Add the soymilk and simmer on a low fire until the potatoes are cooked. Add the lime juice and remove from the heat. Serve with rice.

Serves 3 to 4

Per serving: Calories: 162, Protein: 5 gm., Fat: 6 gm., Carbohydrates: 22 gm.

Mixed Vegetable Curry

1 medium tomato, chopped
1 carrot, chopped
2 medium onions, chopped
1 cup green beans, cut
1 cup cabbage, chopped
1 to 2 cups water
¼ lb tofu, cubed
2 teaspoons oil
1½ teaspoons curry powder
1 teaspoon chili powder
1 teaspoon paprika
½ teaspoon turmeric
1 teaspoon salt

In a medium frying pan, simmer all of the vegetables in the water until the carrot is soft. In a small frying pan, lightly brown the tofu in hot oil. When all of the vegetables are soft, mix in the tofu, curry, chili powder, paprika, turmeric, and salt. Simmer for 15 to 20 minutes. Serve with rice, chapati, and a little yogurt on the side.

Serves 4

Per serving: Calories: 79, Protein: 3 gm., Fat: 3 gm., Carbohydrates: 9 gm.

Kandy Bean Curry

2 cups water
½ cup cracked, dehulled soybeans
    (page 16)
2 tablespoons fresh coconut, grated
2 teaspoons chili powder
2 teaspoons curry powder
1 teaspoon salt
1 teaspoon paprika
½ teaspoon turmeric
1 tablespoon onion, diced
1 teaspoon mustard seeds
2 teaspoons oil
1 medium tomato, diced

Boil 1½ cups water in a small saucepan, add the cracked, dehulled beans, and boil for 20 minutes. Drain the water and reserve for later. Grind the cooked beans to a fine paste in a grain mill. Mix the coconut, chili powder, curry, salt, paprika, and turmeric in a small bowl. In a small saucepan, sauté the onion and mustard seeds in the oil. Add the tomato and the soybean cooking water to the onion mix. Add the dry seasonings and simmer for 5 minutes. Add the soybean paste with another ½ cup of water, and simmer for an additional 30 minutes. Serve with rice and yogurt on the side.

Serves 4

Per serving: Calories: 111, Protein: 4 gm., Fat: 8 gm., Carbohydrates: 5 gm.

Colombo Curry

You can have one of these for a lunch break while swerving through traffic in Colombo. The traffic passes in all shapes and forms through a series of roundabouts. Imagine, three million people and no traffic lights!

¼ lb tempeh, cut into small cubes
1 tablespoon oil
1 medium tomato, chopped
1 tablespoon onion, chopped
1 teaspoon mustard seeds
1 teaspoon oil
1 teaspoon cardamom powder
1 teaspoon curry powder
1 teaspoon chili powder
1 teaspoon salt
¾ cup water

In a small frying pan, brown the tempeh in 1 tablespoon of hot oil. In a medium frying pan, sauté the tomato, onion, and mustard seeds in 1 teaspoon of oil. Add the cardamom, curry, chili powder, and salt to the tomato mixture, then add the water. Stir well and simmer. Add the tempeh, reduce the heat, and cook for 20 minutes. Serve with rice or baked potatoes.

Serves 2 to 3

Per serving: Calories: 164, Protein: 8 gm., Fat: 9 gm., Carbohydrates: 10 gm.

Desserts and Crunchy Snacks

Spicy Soy Nuts

3 cups water
1 cup cracked, dehulled soybeans
     (page 16)
salt
chili powder

Bring the water to a boil, add the dehulled soybeans, and boil for 20 minutes. Drain off the water and dry the blanched beans on paper towels to absorb the excess water. Place the soybeans on a cookie sheet and roast in the oven at 350°F until they turn golden brown. Shake the pan several times during baking to turn the beans. Sprinkle with salt and chili powder to taste. Mix well and serve.

Makes 2 cups

Per ½ cup: Calories: 75, Protein: 6 gm., Fat: 4 gm., Carbohydrates: 4 gm.

Murukku

A great crunchy treat.

¾ cup unbleached white flour
¼ cup full-fat soy flour (page 11)
2 small red onions, grated
1 teaspoon curry powder
2 teaspoons chili powder
1 teaspoon turmeric
salt to taste
oil for frying

Sift together the white flour and soy flour. Mix the onions, curry, chili powder, turmeric, and salt, and add to the flour. Knead to a soft dough by adding ¼ cup warm water a little at a time. Press the dough through a murukku mold (page 9) or a meat grinder, using the smallest holes. Fry in very hot oil. Remove the murukku from the oil when the foam subsides, and drain on paper towels.

Serves 4

Per serving: Calories: 116, Protein: 5 gm., Fat: 1 gm., Carbohydrates: 20 gm.

Nut Sweet

3 cups water
½ cup soybeans
oil for frying
½ cup roasted, ground peanuts
½ cup sugar
½ cup water
½ teaspoon cardamom powder

Bring the water to a boil, add the soybeans, and boil for 20 minutes. Drain and dry the blanched beans on paper towels. Fry handfuls of the blanched soybeans in hot oil until they turn golden brown. With a mortar and pestle grind the roasted soybeans into small pieces, and mix with the peanuts. Combine the sugar and water and boil until a syrupy consistency is reached, then add the cardamom powder. Continue cooking the syrup until a 1 thread consistency is reached (the syrup should hold together like a piece of thread when you lift out the spoon being used to stir it). Add the soy/peanut mixture and mix thoroughly. Pour onto a small oiled cookie sheet or pie pan. Let cool and cut into squares while the candy is still warm.

Makes 20 pieces

Per piece: Calories: 54, Protein: 2 gm., Fat: 2 gm., Carbohydrates: 6 gm.

Coconut Sesame Toffee

1 cup cracked, dehulled soybeans
   (page 16)
½ cup sesame seeds
1 cup dried shredded coconut
1 cup sugar
1 cup water

In a medium frying pan, toast the cracked, dehulled soybeans and sesame seeds until golden brown. Remove from the heat and mix in the coconut. In a medium saucepan, mix the sugar and water, and gently boil until the syrup reaches a 1 thread consistency (the syrup should hold together like a piece of thread when you lift out the spoon being used to stir it). Add the soybean, sesame, and coconut mix to the syrup, and mix thoroughly. Pour into a small oiled baking pan, and spread to a ½-inch thickness. Cut the toffee into pieces while it is still warm.

Makes 20 pieces

Per piece: Calories: 147, Protein: 3 gm., Fat: 9 gm., Carbohydrates: 13 gm.

Watalappam

This is a very popular dessert in Sri Lanka.

½ cup jaggery (page 12) or brown
  sugar
1 cup soymilk
3 eggs
1 teaspoon vanilla
½ teaspoon ground cinnamon
½ teaspoon ground cardamom
½ teaspoon ground mace
¼ teaspoon ground cloves
1 pinch of salt

Dissolve the jaggery or brown sugar in the soymilk. Beat the eggs, add the vanilla, then pour into the soymilk/jaggery mixture. Add the cinnamon, cardamom, mace, cloves, and salt, and stir well. Simmer slowly for 30 minutes. Spoon into small cups or dishes, and serve warm.

Serves 6

Per serving: Calories: 98, Protein: 4 gm., Fat: 4 gm., Carbohydrates: 12 gm.

Soy Dooth
(soymilk, saffron, and nuts)

4 cups soymilk
5 tablespoons sugar
½ teaspoon powdered cardamom
¼ teaspoon saffron
1 tablespoon slivered almonds
1 tablespoon slivered pistachios

Combine the soymilk, sugar, cardamom, and saffron in a medium saucepan. Bring to a boil, lower the heat, and simmer for 2 minutes. Blend the mixture in a blender until it froths. Pour into cups and sprinkle almonds and pistachios over the top. Serve immediately.

Makes approximately 4 cups

Per cup: Calories: 163, Protein: 7 gm., Fat: 7 gm., Carbohydrates: 20 gm.

Rice Aluwa

A delicious, sweet family treat.

⅔ cup rice (or ½ cup rice flour)
¼ cup cracked, dehulled soybeans
(page 16) or 2 tablespoons full-fat
soy flour
½ cup sugar
½ teaspoon cardamom powder
5 cashew nuts, chopped
½ cup scraped jaggery (page 12)
or brown sugar
½ cup water

Rinse the rice, drain, and roast in a medium frying pan or oven until slightly brown. Grind to a flour with mortar & pestle or grain or coffee mill. Blanch the soybeans in boiling water for 20 minutes, drain, and dry on trays in the oven at 350°F. Grind to a flour with mortar and pestle or grain or coffee mill. Mix the rice and soybean flours, cardamom, and cashew nuts. Combine the jaggery or brown sugar and boil until the syrup is a 1 thread consistency (the syrup should hold together like a piece of thread when you lift out the spoon being used to stir it). Remove from the heat and add the flour mixture. Mix thoroughly and flatten on a greased surface. Cut into pieces while warm, let cool, and serve.

Makes 24 pieces

Per piece: Calories: 46, Protein: 1 gm., Fat: 0 gm., Carbohydrates: 10 gm.

The Photographs

Continued . . .

Continued . . .

Index

About Plenty

Plenty was created by the Farm community in Tennessee in 1974 as an expression of the Farm's desire to do more than just take care of itself. Independent of governments, political agencies, or religious institutions, Plenty represents the belief that if we wisely protect, manage, and share the earth's resources, there will be enough for all—plenty.

The process of building a town from the ground up provided Farm members with skills that later became the basis for technical assistance offered by Plenty. Over it's 21 year history, Plenty's work has spanned a wide range of activities in many countries and with many peoples—from primary health care training in Lesotho, southern Africa, and Washington, D.C. to establishing potable water systems for rural villages in Guatemala; from community-based agriculture at the Pine Ridge reservation in South Dakota to micro-enterprise development in the Caribbean.

Plenty shared in the first Right Livelihood Award (the alternative Nobel prize) presented in Stockholm, Sweden in 1980, and Plenty's free, volunteer ambulance service and paramedic training program in the South Bronx received the Jefferson Award for community service in 1981.

Plenty has learned over the years what real development is about—helping people directly, in ways *they* want to be helped. Plenty's role is to act in partnership with people trying to implement their own good ideas about community development.

Plenty's focus is on indigenous people and the environment, and active programs in 1995 include the Soy Utilization Training and Promotion (SUTAP), the work of which is discussed in this book; Indigenous Women's Economic Development (IWED); the Natural Rights Center (NRC); the Environmental Resource Center of Oregon (ERC); and Kids to the Country.

Plenty's Indigenous Women's Economic Development program provides technical assistance to artisan cooperatives and markets and distributes their products through the De Colores Fair Trade Center in Davis,

California. IWED gives the artisans a fair price for their work (the price that the producers determine), and offers technical assistance in the form of product design, management training, coalition building, consumer education, and market expansion. In addition, IWED has been instrumental in the on-going formation and implementation of North American "fair trade" policies and in the development of an international alternative trade organization, the Fair Trade Federation.

Plenty sponsors a number of active environmental programs in North America. The Natural Rights Center, which has its headquarters at the Farm, and the Environmental Resource Center of Oregon, maintain active litigation in support of local, national, and international environmental initiatives concerning treaties on global climate change, deepwell injection, nuclear disarmament, endangered species, judicial reform, recycling, carrying capacity, wetlands, Nuclear Winter, forest conservation, and atomic veterans, to name a few. Plenty also sponsors the Ecovillage Training Center, a project of the Global Village Institute.

Kids to the Country brings a mix of young people from inner cities, and homeless or refugee families to the Farm to experience fresh air, horseback riding, craft-making, swimming and canoeing, and a host of other activities. Along with country living, the kids are exposed to non-violent conflict resolution and environmental appreciation which they carry with them when they return home.

Plenty serves as the fiscal sponsor for other projects which fit under Plenty's general philosophy and guidelines. Plenty is a 501c3 charitable organization managed by an Executive Staff and Volunteer Board, and assisted by a Council of Advisors. The Plenty Bulletin is mailed quarterly to all donors. For more information, please contact:

Plenty
P.O. Box 394
Summertown TN 38483 USA.

Tel: (615) 964-4864.

E-mail: plentyusa@MCIMail.com

Ask your store to carry these books, or you may order directly from:

The Book Publishing Company
P.O. Box 99
Summertown, TN 38483

Or call: 1-800-695-2241
Please add $2.50 per book for shipping

Almost-No Fat Cookbook $10.95

American Harvest 11.95

Burgers 'n Fries 'n Cinnamon Buns 6.95

Cookin' Healthy with One Foot Out the Door 8.95

Cooking with Gluten and Seitan 7.95

Ecological Cooking: Recipes to Save the Planet 10.95

Fabulous Beans 9.95

From A Traditional Greek Kitchen 9.95

Good Time Eatin' in Cajun Country 9.95

George Bernard Shaw Vegetarian Cookbook 8.95

Holiday Diet Book 9.95

Indian Vegetarian Cooking at Your House 12.95

Instead of Chicken, Instead of Turkey 9.95

Judy Brown's Guide to Natural Foods Cooking 10.95

Kids Can Cook 9.95

Murrieta Hot Springs Vegetarian Cookbook 8.95